BIBLE PROMISES FOR MOMS

Heidi St. John

BIBLE PROMISES

for Moms

TYNDALE
MOMENTUM®

The nonfiction imprint of
Tyndale House Publishers, Inc.

Visit Tyndale online at www.tyndale.com.

Visit Tyndale Momentum online at www.tyndalemomentum.com.

Visit the author's website at www.heidistjohn.com.

TYNDALE, *Tyndale Momentum*, and Tyndale's quill logo are registered trademarks of Tyndale House Publishers, Inc. The Tyndale Momentum logo is a trademark of Tyndale House Publishers, Inc. Tyndale Momentum is the nonfiction imprint of Tyndale House Publishers, Inc., Carol Stream, Illinois.

Bible Promises for Moms

Designed by Julie Chen

Edited by Deborah King

Published in association with William K. Jensen Literary Agency, 119 Bampton Court, Eugene, Oregon 97404

For information about special discounts for bulk purchases, please contact Tyndale House Publishers at csresponse@tyndale.com, or call 1-800-323-9400.

ISBN 978-1-4964-1272-0

Printed in the United States of America

25	24	23	22	21	20	19
8	7	6	5	4	3	

This book is dedicated to my beautiful daughters:

Savannah

Sierra

Summer

Sydney

&

Saylor

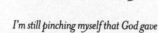

I'm still pinching myself that God gave

your dad and me five daughters. Such a gift!

When life is hard, precious girls, lean in to Jesus.

I promise, His promises are for you.

And so am I.

You are loved.

Contents

Introduction

I am confident I will see the LORD's goodness
while I am here in the land of the living.
Wait patiently for the LORD. Be brave and courageous.
PSALM 27:13-14

MOTHERHOOD. It's two parts exhilaration and one part exasperation—or is it the other way around? I suppose it depends, doesn't it? If you're nodding with me, lean in close, because it's time to change our perspective. I wrote *Bible Promises for Moms* for every mother who needs to hear God's wisdom for parenting in a world that values human wisdom. The world will tell you that God's Word is "outdated" and "irrelevant" when it comes to the challenges of modern motherhood. Don't listen. God's Word is as relevant and life-giving today as it was when it was written.

In the pages of this book, you'll find hope in the midst of heartache, spiritual salve for your soul, and supernatural strength for your mother's heart. In short—you'll find *hope*. No matter where you are in your mothering journey, God's mercies are for you. He is your hope. He'll meet you in the dark of night when your strength (and your perspective) is gone. He'll steady your heart and renew your mind as you meet new challenges and throughout the ever-changing seasons of motherhood. We have hope because God's promises never fail. His wisdom is for the ages and, I think, especially this one. Oh, how we need to hear His gentle and wise voice right now.

I'm so glad that God's promises don't change. They don't depend on our strength or our performance. They're an anchor for our souls and a sure foundation upon which we can start to build and shape the character of the next generation.

One glimpse of things from God's perspective can change ours.

Can you hear Him? He's whispering, "I love you" through the pages of the Bible. He sees your struggle and says, "I'm right here by your side."

Lean in to His promises today. God has you in His grasp. Lean in and ask for His help as you seek God's perspective with your whole heart. The Bible displays the heart of the Father on every page. You'll find everything covered in this book, from abandonment to yearning—because God's promises are for you. You can use *Bible Promises for Moms* to look things up topically, whether as part of your daily devotions or to counsel another mom. No matter how you use it, I pray your heart will be steadied and your load lightened by the beautiful promises of God.

Shhh. Quiet down, world. I'm leaning in to hear the still, small voice of my Creator. Lean in with me, precious mom. Let's soak up every beautiful word of truth from the Bible that we can.

His Word is true. His promises never fail.

Spring 2019

Heidi St. John

Abandonment —

WHEN YOU FEEL THAT GOD HAS LEFT YOU . . .

Those who know your name trust in you,
>   for you, O LORD, do not abandon those who
>   search for you.

PSALM 9:10

**WHEN YOU WONDER IF THERE IS ANYTHING
YOU CAN DO THAT WILL CAUSE GOD TO LEAVE . . .**

God has said,
"I will never fail you.
>   I will never abandon you."

HEBREWS 13:5

Adoption —

WHEN YOU NEED TO HEAR THAT GOD LOVES ADOPTION . . .

Pure and genuine religion in the sight of God the
Father means caring for orphans and widows in their
distress.

JAMES 1:27

**WHEN YOU NEED REASSURANCE OF
YOUR ADOPTION INTO GOD'S FAMILY . . .**

We believers also groan, even though we have the
Holy Spirit within us as a foretaste of future glory,

for we long for our bodies to be released from sin and suffering. We, too, wait with eager hope for the day when God will give us our full rights as his adopted children, including the new bodies he has promised us.

ROMANS 8:23

You are no longer a slave but God's own child. And since you are his child, God has made you his heir.

GALATIANS 4:7

**WHEN YOUR ADOPTED CHILD NEEDS
REASSURANCE OF GOD'S PLANS FOR THEIR LIFE . . .**

You saw me before I was born.
    Every day of my life was recorded in your book.
Every moment was laid out
    before a single day had passed.

PSALM 139:16

"I know the plans I have for you," says the LORD. "They are plans for good and not for disaster, to give you a future and a hope."

JEREMIAH 29:11

Anger

WHEN YOU ARE WORRIED THAT GOD IS ANGRY WITH YOU . . .

His anger lasts only a moment,
    but his favor lasts a lifetime!

Weeping may last through the night,
    but joy comes with the morning.

PSALM 30:5

The LORD is compassionate and merciful,
    slow to get angry and filled with unfailing love.

PSALM 103:8

WHEN YOU'RE ANGRY AND DON'T KNOW WHAT TO DO...

"Don't sin by letting anger control you." Don't let the
sun go down while you are still angry.

EPHESIANS 4:26

Understand this, my dear brothers and sisters: You
must all be quick to listen, slow to speak, and slow
to get angry. Human anger does not produce the
righteousness God desires.

JAMES 1:19-20

WHEN YOU NEED TO TALK WITH YOUR CHILDREN ABOUT ANGER...

A gentle answer deflects anger,
    but harsh words make tempers flare.

PROVERBS 15:1

Assurance

WHEN YOU OR YOUR CHILD NEEDS ASSURANCE OF SALVATION...

As for me, I know that my Redeemer lives,
    and he will stand upon the earth at last.

And after my body has decayed,
    yet in my body I will see God!
I will see him for myself.
    Yes, I will see him with my own eyes.
    I am overwhelmed at the thought!
    JOB 19:25-27

God has given us his Spirit as proof that we live in him
and he in us. Furthermore, we have seen with our own
eyes and now testify that the Father sent his Son to
be the Savior of the world. All who declare that Jesus
is the Son of God have God living in them, and they
live in God. We know how much God loves us, and we
have put our trust in his love.

    God is love, and all who live in love live in
God, and God lives in them.
    1 JOHN 4:13-16

I have written this to you who believe in the name
of the Son of God, so that you may know you have
eternal life.
    1 JOHN 5:13

Babies ⟶

People often ask my husband and me if we planned to have
seven children, and I love to answer that question because it
tells the story of a gentle shift in our views. I was forty-one when I
became pregnant with our seventh baby—not something I would

have ever thought I wanted when I was younger. Early in our marriage, we saw children as a blessing, but I'll admit—the culture's low view of children had clouded our perspective. We worried about the financial commitment. At times, all I could see in front of me was a demanding baby and an ungrateful toddler. Can you relate? If so, take a deep breath with me as we embrace what God says is good. His love for children is clear.

When I began to seek God's heart for children, my heart changed. I began to see that *babies are a blessing.* Embracing God's heart for children changed our lives. Sure, there have been difficult times. Many of them. In fact, my hunch is that you, too, may be tired and wonder if what you're doing is worth it—but precious mom, know that it is.

God's ways are always good. In answer to our prayers, God gave us a baby in our forties. Saylor Jane's arrival in God's timeline was in keeping with His good plan for us. Our lives have been enriched beyond our wildest dreams by this little "caboose baby" that the Lord gave us out of the goodness of His heart.

Planned or unplanned, fostered or adopted, special needs or perfectly healthy, God says children are a blessing and a reward. Let's choose to see these precious ones the way God sees them—and experience the blessing that comes with embracing what God embraces.

WHEN YOU'RE STRUGGLING WITH AN UNPLANNED PREGNANCY . . .

Children are a gift from the LORD;
> they are a reward from him.
PSALM 127:3

I can do everything through Christ, who gives me
strength.

PHILIPPIANS 4:13

Whatever is good and perfect is a gift coming down
to us from God our Father, who created all the lights
in the heavens. He never changes or casts a shifting
shadow. He chose to give birth to us by giving us his
true word. And we, out of all creation, became his
prized possession.

JAMES 1:17-18

WHEN YOU NEED TO REMEMBER GOD'S HEART FOR THOSE YET TO BE BORN . . .

You brought me safely from my mother's womb
     and led me to trust you at my mother's breast.
I was thrust into your arms at my birth.
     You have been my God from the moment I was
          born.

PSALM 22:9-10

You made all the delicate, inner parts of my body
     and knit me together in my mother's womb.
Thank you for making me so wonderfully complex!
     Your workmanship is marvelous—how well I know it.

PSALM 139:13-14

WHEN YOUR PRAYERS FOR A CHILD HAVE BEEN ANSWERED . . .

I asked the LORD to give me this boy, and he has
granted my request.

1 SAMUEL 1:27

Belonging

WHEN YOU NEED TO KNOW THAT YOU ARE GOD'S PRECIOUS CHILD . . .

If we live, it's to honor the Lord. And if we die, it's to honor the Lord. So whether we live or die, we belong to the Lord.

ROMANS 14:8

You are all children of the light and of the day; we don't belong to darkness and night.

1 THESSALONIANS 5:5

See how very much our Father loves us, for he calls us his children, and that is what we are!

1 JOHN 3:1

Bible

WHEN YOU NEED TO REMEMBER THE
IMPORTANCE OF STUDYING SCRIPTURE . . .

The word of God is alive and powerful. It is sharper than the sharpest two-edged sword, cutting between soul and spirit, between joint and marrow. It exposes our innermost thoughts and desires.

HEBREWS 4:12

All Scripture is inspired by God and is useful to teach us what is true and to make us realize what is wrong in our lives. It corrects us when we are wrong and teaches

us to do what is right. God uses it to prepare and equip
his people to do every good work.

2 TIMOTHY 3:16-17

WHEN YOU WANT YOUR CHILDREN TO SEE
THE BLESSING OF FOLLOWING GOD'S WORD . . .

How can a young person stay pure?
By obeying your word.

PSALM 119:9

Jesus replied, "But even more blessed are all who hear
the word of God and put it into practice."

LUKE 11:28

Birth ⟶

WHEN YOUR CHILD ASKS IF GOD PLANNED THEIR BIRTH . . .

You made all the delicate, inner parts of my body
and knit me together in my mother's womb.
Thank you for making me so wonderfully complex!
Your workmanship is marvelous—how well I know it.
You watched me as I was being formed in utter seclusion,
as I was woven together in the dark of the womb.
You saw me before I was born.
Every day of my life was recorded in your book.
Every moment was laid out
before a single day had passed.

PSALM 139:13-16

WHEN CHILDBIRTH FRIGHTENS YOU . . .

When I am afraid,
  I will put my trust in you.
  PSALM 56:3

From the ends of the earth,
  I cry to you for help
  when my heart is overwhelmed.
Lead me to the towering rock of safety.
  PSALM 61:2

Blessing

WHEN YOU WANT TO SEE FRUIT FROM YOUR MOTHERING . . .

How great is the goodness
  you have stored up for those who fear you.
You lavish it on those who come to you for protection,
  blessing them before the watching world.
  PSALM 31:19

Blessed are those who trust in the LORD
  and have made the LORD their hope and confidence.
They are like trees planted along a riverbank,
  with roots that reach deep into the water.
Such trees are not bothered by the heat
  or worried by long months of drought.
Their leaves stay green,
  and they never stop producing fruit.
  JEREMIAH 17:7-8

Study this Book of Instruction continually. Meditate on it day and night so you will be sure to obey everything written in it. Only then will you prosper and succeed in all you do.

JOSHUA 1:8

The LORD God is our sun and our shield.
    He gives us grace and glory.
The LORD will withhold no good thing
    from those who do what is right.

PSALM 84:11

Let's not get tired of doing what is good. At just the right time we will reap a harvest of blessing if we don't give up.

GALATIANS 6:9

Bullies

WHEN YOUR CHILD WANTS TO GET EVEN WITH A BULLY . . .

To you who are willing to listen, I say, love your enemies! Do good to those who hate you. Bless those who curse you. Pray for those who hurt you.

LUKE 6:27-28

Do all that you can to live in peace with everyone.
    Dear friends, never take revenge. Leave that to the righteous anger of God. For the Scriptures say,

"I will take revenge;
    I will pay them back,"
    says the LORD.
    ROMANS 12:18-19

WHEN YOU AND YOUR CHILD ARE STRUGGLING TO FORGIVE . . .

I say, love your enemies! Pray for those who persecute
you! In that way, you will be acting as true children of
your Father in heaven. For he gives his sunlight to both
the evil and the good, and he sends rain on the just
and the unjust alike.
    MATTHEW 5:44-45

Burnout

I had spoken eight times in thirty hours and then just barely
caught my flight back to the Pacific Northwest. After nine hours
in the air and a two-hour layover, I was close to home at last,
grateful that my husband was driving along the nearly deserted
I-5 freeway at midnight on a Sunday night. The last half hour
on the plane had given me a chance to collect my thoughts and
get my to-do list ready for Monday morning. My heart sank as I
mentally reviewed the laundry, homeschooling, shopping, and
the dozen other things waiting to be done at home when it hit
me: I was running on fumes. Tears filled my eyes—until I heard
the gentle voice of the Holy Spirit saying, "Stop and rest."

Do you need to stop and rest? Most moms I know run

on fumes from time to time—and here's the thing we need to remember: the Lord is faithful to provide us with times of refreshment when we are faithful to listen for His voice. Sometimes we simply need to draw away from the tyranny of all that needs to be done and spend some time alone with God. He is faithful. Instead of rushing right into my to-do list, I quieted my heart. Taking time to slow down and listen for the voice of God can change your perspective and renew your spirit. Are you burned out? God says, "Be still."

WHEN YOUR MOTHER-HEART NEEDS TO SLOW DOWN . . .

God blessed the seventh day and declared it holy, because it was the day when he rested from all his work of creation.

GENESIS 2:3

Those who trust in the LORD will find new strength.
    They will soar high on wings like eagles.
They will run and not grow weary.
    They will walk and not faint.

ISAIAH 40:31

Jesus said, "Let's go off by ourselves to a quiet place and rest awhile." He said this because there were so many people coming and going that Jesus and his apostles didn't even have time to eat.

    So they left by boat for a quiet place, where they could be alone.

MARK 6:31-32

Children

WHEN YOU WONDER HOW GOD FEELS ABOUT CHILDREN . . .

Children are a gift from the LORD;
　　they are a reward from him.
Children born to a young man
　　are like arrows in a warrior's hands.
How joyful is the man whose quiver is full of them!
　　He will not be put to shame when he confronts his
　　　　accusers at the city gates.

PSALM 127:3-5

WHEN YOU NEED TO REMEMBER HOW TO REALLY HEAR FROM GOD . . .

The disciples came to Jesus and asked, "Who is greatest
in the Kingdom of Heaven?"

　　Jesus called a little child to him and put the
child among them. Then he said, "I tell you the
truth, unless you turn from your sins and become
like little children, you will never get into the
Kingdom of Heaven."

MATTHEW 18:1-3

WHEN YOUR CHILDREN NEED TO SEE THEIR WORTH IN GOD'S EYES . . .

[Jesus said,] "Anyone who welcomes a little child like
this on my behalf welcomes me, and anyone who
welcomes me welcomes not only me but also my Father
who sent me."

MARK 9:37

Jesus called for the children and said to the disciples, "Let the children come to me. Don't stop them! For the Kingdom of God belongs to those who are like these children."

LUKE 18:16

WHEN YOU'RE PREPARING TO GIVE BIRTH . . .

It will be like a woman suffering the pains of labor. When her child is born, her anguish gives way to joy because she has brought a new baby into the world.

JOHN 16:21

Confidence

We live in a world where every self-help book and Internet expert touts the importance of self-confidence. We moms often read articles about self-image and self-confidence, even self-worth, trying to make ourselves feel better about ourselves, trying to convince ourselves we're good mothers. But do you see the error? The focus is on *self*! As daughters of the King, our focus should not be on self but rather on the Savior. Because of Jesus, I can boldly say that I am loved. Because I've been adopted into God's family, I can be confident that my worth is immeasurable and that my future is secure. Place your confidence in the Lord and His Word, precious mom. God will never fail you. He who began a good work in you will finish it. Good things are coming!

WHEN YOUR CONFIDENCE HAS BEEN MISPLACED . . .

Trust in the LORD with all your heart;
>   do not depend on your own understanding.
Seek his will in all you do,
>   and he will show you which path to take.
>   PROVERBS 3:5-6

WHEN YOUR CHILD NEEDS TO KNOW WHERE TO FIND CONFIDENCE . . .

Though I am surrounded by troubles,
>   you will protect me from the anger of my enemies.
You reach out your hand,
>   and the power of your right hand saves me.
>   PSALM 138:7

WHEN YOU WONDER IF GOD IS LISTENING . . .

We are confident that he hears us whenever we ask for anything that pleases him. And since we know he hears us when we make our requests, we also know that he will give us what we ask for.
>   1 JOHN 5:14-15

Contentment

WHEN YOU FEEL UNHAPPY WITH WHAT YOU HAVE . . .

Not that I was ever in need, for I have learned how to be content with whatever I have. I know how to live on almost nothing or with everything. I have learned the

secret of living in every situation, whether it is with a
full stomach or empty, with plenty or little.

PHILIPPIANS 4:11-12

WHEN YOU NEED TO REMEMBER THAT
GOD KNOWS WHAT YOU NEED . . .

Your heavenly Father already knows all your needs.
Seek the Kingdom of God above all else, and live
righteously, and he will give you everything you
need.

MATTHEW 6:32-33

We are confident that he hears us whenever we ask for
anything that pleases him. And since we know he hears
us when we make our requests, we also know that he
will give us what we ask for.

1 JOHN 5:14-15

Courage

My little girl was still in elementary school when she stumbled
upon a big, bold lie at our small town library. The lie was being
told through the pages of a beautifully illustrated children's
book. "Mommy?" Her innocent brown eyes looked piercingly
into mine. "Can I change into a boy?" My palms got sweaty,
and my heart raced as I tried to take notice of our surround-
ings. I wondered who overheard her question. Of course, she
knew the answer . . . but the beautiful pictures made the lie

seem appealing. Isn't that how Satan has operated from the beginning of time? He's mastered the art of the beautiful lie—and as a result, parents are facing hard questions from their kids.

Hard questions require hard answers and, in this case, hard truth. Have you ever had to tell your child a hard truth? The culture today is warring against the truth of God's Word about everything from our personal identity to the value of human life. As followers of Jesus, our first responsibility to our children is to be ambassadors for Him. And these days, that takes courage. Are your children asking you difficult questions? Take them to the Word of God. Have the courage to engage with your children, even when it's hard. The Bible has the answers that you need for every situation. If you're struggling to have courage, take heart! The Lord of heaven's armies is by your side!

WHEN YOU FEEL FRIGHTENED AND BLINDSIDED BY A BIG PROBLEM . . .

This is my command—be strong and courageous! Do not be afraid or discouraged. For the LORD your God is with you wherever you go.

JOSHUA 1:9

I hold you by your right hand—
    I, the LORD your God.
And I say to you,
    "Don't be afraid. I am here to help you."

ISAIAH 41:13

WHEN YOU OR YOUR CHILD NEEDS
TO KNOW WHO THE REAL ENEMY IS . . .

We are not fighting against flesh-and-blood enemies, but against evil rulers and authorities of the unseen world, against mighty powers in this dark world, and against evil spirits in the heavenly places.

EPHESIANS 6:12

Death

WHEN YOUR CHILD IS FEARFUL OF DEATH . . .

When our dying bodies have been transformed into bodies that will never die, this Scripture will be fulfilled:

"Death is swallowed up in victory.
O death, where is your victory?
    O death, where is your sting?"

For sin is the sting that results in death, and the law gives sin its power. But thank God! He gives us victory over sin and death through our Lord Jesus Christ.

1 CORINTHIANS 15:54-57

WHEN YOU NEED FAITH TO BELIEVE THAT DEATH IS NOT THE END . . .

Jesus told her, "I am the resurrection and the life. Anyone who believes in me will live, even after dying. Everyone who lives in me and believes in me will never ever die."

JOHN 11:25-26

Decisions ⟶

WHEN YOU DON'T KNOW WHERE TO START . . .

Trust in the LORD with all your heart;
do not depend on your own understanding.
Seek his will in all you do,
and he will show you which path to take.

PROVERBS 3:5-6

If you need wisdom, ask our generous God, and
he will give it to you. He will not rebuke you for
asking.

JAMES 1:5

WHEN YOUR WEARY HEART NEEDS DIRECTION . . .

The instructions of the LORD are perfect,
reviving the soul.
The decrees of the LORD are trustworthy,
making wise the simple.
The commandments of the LORD are right,
bringing joy to the heart.
The commands of the LORD are clear,
giving insight for living.

PSALM 19:7-8

Depression —

Depression affects most women at some point in their lives. I know about this battle firsthand, as I've had my own struggle to get out of the pit of anxiety. So hear me—it's not a sin to talk to your physician or to use a prescription to help if that's what's needed. But we also need to seek the help of the Great Physician. God's healing is real—and *His perspective is necessary for every kind of healing*. Are you feeling depressed? Meditate on God's Word! Turn up the worship music! Turn your sorrow into praise. Look heavenward with me, sweet mom, and let's declare together that God's plans for us and for our children are good. Let's sing out loud of His healing and of the hope we have because of Jesus. No, it's not a case of "positive thinking" but a decision to choose joy and refuse to be defined by our suffering. Jesus has made a way. Let's walk in it!

WHEN YOU'RE STRUGGLING WITH YOUR THOUGHTS . . .

Dear brothers and sisters, one final thing. Fix your thoughts on what is true, and honorable, and right, and pure, and lovely, and admirable. Think about things that are excellent and worthy of praise.

PHILIPPIANS 4:8

Since you have been raised to new life with Christ, set your sights on the realities of heaven, where Christ sits in the place of honor at God's right hand. Think about the things of heaven, not the things of earth.

COLOSSIANS 3:1-2

WHEN SADNESS OVERWHELMS YOU . . .

Why am I discouraged?
    Why is my heart so sad?
I will put my hope in God!
    I will praise him again—
    my Savior and my God!
    PSALM 42:11

Discipline

**WHEN YOU NEED TO BE REMINDED
THAT DISCIPLINE IS WORTH IT . . .**

Direct your children onto the right path,
    and when they are older, they will not leave it.
    PROVERBS 22:6

To discipline a child produces wisdom,
    but a mother is disgraced by an undisciplined child.
    PROVERBS 29:15

**WHEN YOUR HEART LONGS TO SEE
YOUR CHILDREN EXPERIENCE GOD'S BLESSING . . .**

Honor your father and mother. Then you will live
a long, full life in the land the LORD your God is
giving you.
    EXODUS 20:12

Do not provoke your children to anger by the way you treat them. Rather, bring them up with the discipline and instruction that comes from the Lord.

EPHESIANS 6:4

Discouragement

Our finished basement had just flooded—for the second time. I was bone-weary, exhausted and discouraged beyond words as we dragged furniture out onto the lawn and pulled up soaked carpeting and padding—again. I cried out to the Lord in the midst of my discouragement—but unbeknownst to me, He was already at work. Neighbors came with warm meals; men came with shovels. One precious mom even brought over a pizza bar, to the delight of our kids. As we ate homemade pizza surrounded by ruined furniture, I heard the Lord's gentle reminder: "I am here." Because of our flooded basement, we made new friends. Because our oven went out, another mom saw an opportunity to bless us—and that pizza dinner investment is still paying friendship dividends today. Weary mom . . . when we cry out to the Lord, He always hears our cries. His ways are beyond our ways, and sometimes they include a hot meal in the middle of the mess. Don't let your heart *stay* discouraged. God is up to something good!

WHEN YOU NEED TO BE REMINDED THAT GOD HEARS YOU . . .

The LORD hears his people when they call to him
    for help.
    He rescues them from all their troubles.
The LORD is close to the brokenhearted;
    he rescues those whose spirits are crushed.
The righteous person faces many troubles,
    but the LORD comes to the rescue each time.
    PSALM 34:17-19

WHEN YOUR MOTHER'S HEART IS ACHING . . .

Give your burdens to the LORD,
    and he will take care of you.
    He will not permit the godly to slip and fall.
    PSALM 55:22

He heals the brokenhearted
    and bandages their wounds.
    PSALM 147:3

Don't be afraid, for I am with you.
    Don't be discouraged, for I am your God.
I will strengthen you and help you.
    I will hold you up with my victorious right hand.
    ISAIAH 41:10

WHEN YOU FEEL ANYTHING BUT STRONG . . .

Those who trust in the LORD will find new strength.
    They will soar high on wings like eagles.

They will run and not grow weary.
    They will walk and not faint.
    ISAIAH 40:31

Doubt

**WHEN YOU DOUBT YOUR ABILITY TO
BE THE MOM YOU WANT TO BE . . .**

God has not given us a spirit of fear and timidity, but
of power, love, and self-discipline.
    2 TIMOTHY 1:7

WHEN DOUBT BECOMES YOUR INNER VOICE . . .

I pray that from his glorious, unlimited resources he will
empower you with inner strength through his Spirit.
    EPHESIANS 3:16

Education

For much of my adult life, I've been immersed in homeschooling.
I began homeschooling (quite by accident, but that's a story for
another day) more than twenty years ago. Over the years, I've
noticed something about education: it can easily become an
idol. Public school, private school, home school—every type of
education has pitfalls for parents. It's easy for parents to focus
on the world's idea of what education should look like. We can

become overly concerned with the three Rs and miss teaching our children about the narrow road that God says leads to life. So no matter how you choose to educate your children, remember this: the Bible promises us that students will be like their teachers (see Luke 6:40). What are your children's teachers like? What are we like as their primary teachers? Remember, we can't pass on what we don't possess.

So before you ensure that your children know math and science, make sure they know that they were created on purpose with a purpose. In other words, make sure your children know how much God loves them. Knowing who we are in Christ and learning about our Creator's heart prepares us for a lifetime of gaining not just knowledge, but wisdom.

WHEN YOU NEED TO BE REMINDED OF THE BLESSING THAT COMES FROM GODLY INSTRUCTION . . .

Commit yourselves wholeheartedly to these words of mine. Tie them to your hands and wear them on your forehead as reminders. Teach them to your children. Talk about them when you are at home and when you are on the road, when you are going to bed and when you are getting up. Write them on the doorposts of your house and on your gates, so that as long as the sky remains above the earth, you and your children may flourish in the land the LORD swore to give your ancestors.

DEUTERONOMY 11:18-21

Direct your children onto the right path,
　　and when they are older, they will not leave it.
PROVERBS 22:6

I will teach all your children,
    and they will enjoy great peace.
    ISAIAH 54:13

Emotions ⟶

Few things feel better than a deep belly laugh or a cleansing, refreshing cry. Emotions are nothing to suppress or fear, but we don't want to be controlled by them either. If you're like me, there are days when you experience every emotion imaginable between breakfast and bedtime. The Bible reminds us that Jesus was tempted in all the same ways that we are. If you're riding one of those emotional roller coasters right now, remember that Jesus understands. He turned to God for help, setting the example for the rest of us. Instead of being ruled by our emotions, let's ask God to help us stay in control of them. Through the gracious and generous help of the Holy Spirit, our emotions can be both embraced and enjoyed.

**WHEN YOU NEED TO REMEMBER THAT
EMOTIONS ARE NOT THE BOSS OF YOU . . .**

Do not let sin control the way you live; do not give in to sinful desires.
    ROMANS 6:12

Do not provoke your children to anger by the way you treat them. Rather, bring them up with the discipline and instruction that comes from the Lord.

EPHESIANS 6:4

WHEN YOU NEED TO REMEMBER THAT THIS LIFE IS SHORT . . .

Our present troubles are small and won't last very long. Yet they produce for us a glory that vastly outweighs them and will last forever!

2 CORINTHIANS 4:17

Encouragement

WHEN YOU'VE FORGOTTEN THAT GOD IS OUR ENCOURAGER . . .

All praise to God, the Father of our Lord Jesus Christ. God is our merciful Father and the source of all comfort. He comforts us in all our troubles so that we can comfort others. When they are troubled, we will be able to give them the same comfort God has given us.

2 CORINTHIANS 1:3-4

WHEN YOU NEED TO REMEMBER TO ENCOURAGE YOUR KIDS . . .

Let us think of ways to motivate one another to acts of love and good works. And let us not neglect our meeting together, as some people do, but encourage one another, especially now that the day of his return is drawing near.

HEBREWS 10:24-25

Endurance

Perhaps you've heard the old line, "How do you eat an elephant?" The answer, of course, is simple: "One bite at a time." Sometimes, that "elephant" is the oh-so-daily job of parenting. It's exhausting. We often want to quit, or we turn to schools, pastors, or friends to tackle the tough job of teaching and training our children. Weariness sets in, and we're tempted to lose interest or disengage. Can I encourage you? Don't do it. Don't give in. Endure. Persevere. The Lord is your help, and your kids are worth every ounce of energy that you put into them. The Bible encourages us that if we persist, if we don't grow weary and give up, if we run the race that's been set before us with endurance, if we plant and tend our fields, in due season we will reap a harvest. That's how we walk out all that God has for us . . . with endurance and perseverance. Don't give up! Don't quit. Endure. God is faithful.

WHEN YOU NEED TO HEAR THAT GOD IS PLEASED WHEN YOU HANG IN THERE . . .

We proudly tell God's other churches about your endurance and faithfulness in all the persecutions and hardships you are suffering.

2 THESSALONIANS 1:4

WHEN YOU WONDER IF YOU'RE MAKING A DIFFERENCE . . .

Let's not get tired of doing what is good. At just the right time we will reap a harvest of blessing if we don't give up.

GALATIANS 6:9

WHEN YOU NEED ENCOURAGEMENT TO STAY IN THE FIGHT . . .

Let us run with endurance the race God has set before us. We do this by keeping our eyes on Jesus, the champion who initiates and perfects our faith. . . . Think of all the hostility he endured from sinful people; then you won't become weary and give up.

HEBREWS 12:1-3

Energy

WHEN YOUR ENERGY IS GONE AND YOU THINK IT'S UP TO YOU TO FIND IT . . .

The Holy Spirit produces this kind of fruit in our lives: love, joy, peace, patience, kindness, goodness, faithfulness, gentleness, and self-control.

GALATIANS 5:22-23

God is working in you, giving you the desire and the power to do what pleases him.

PHILIPPIANS 2:13

Eternity ⌁

WHEN YOUR CHILDREN NEED A REMINDER
THAT GOD OFFERS ETERNAL LIFE . . .

This is the way to have eternal life—to know you, the
only true God, and Jesus Christ, the one you sent
to earth.

JOHN 17:3

The wages of sin is death, but the free gift of God is
eternal life through Christ Jesus our Lord.

ROMANS 6:23

WHEN YOUR MOTHER'S HEART FORGETS
THAT YOU ARE A WORK IN PROGRESS . . .

I am certain that God, who began the good work
within you, will continue his work until it is finally
finished on the day when Christ Jesus returns.

PHILIPPIANS 1:6

Faith ⌁

WHEN YOU'VE FORGOTTEN WHERE TO LOOK . . .

Let us run with endurance the race God has set
before us. We do this by keeping our eyes on Jesus,
the champion who initiates and perfects our faith.
Because of the joy awaiting him, he endured the cross,

disregarding its shame. Now he is seated in the place of honor beside God's throne.

HEBREWS 12:1-2

**WHEN YOUR MOTHER'S HEART NEEDS
TO REMEMBER WHAT GOD CAN DO . . .**

"You don't have enough faith," Jesus told them. "I tell you the truth, if you had faith even as small as a mustard seed, you could say to this mountain, 'Move from here to there,' and it would move. Nothing would be impossible."

MATTHEW 17:20

**WHEN YOU NEED TO REMEMBER THAT FAITH
INVOLVES BELIEVING WHAT WE DO NOT YET SEE . . .**

Faith shows the reality of what we hope for; it is the evidence of things we cannot see.

HEBREWS 11:1

Family

My husband and I have experienced our greatest trials and our greatest joys in the context of raising our seven children. For some of those years we've also enjoyed the blessing of living in an extended family with some of my siblings and with my husband's parents. You see, God is the author of families. Families were His idea. His heart is to take orphans and put them in families. In some cases that means He places those who were once far from God as adopted sons and daughters into God's family. In others it means He orchestrates literal adoptions. And in others He entrusts children to a husband and wife to raise. No matter what your family looks like, know that within the circle of those relationships God intends for you to find joy, peace, and hope as you experience love and intimacy. Family is His idea and He has given it as a gift to you. Even in the sometimes crazy, free-wheeling, seemingly out-of-control days . . . it's a gift. Treasure your family.

WHEN YOU NEED TO LOOK FOR GOD'S GIFTING IN YOUR CHILDREN . . .

God has given each of you a gift from his great variety of spiritual gifts. Use them well to serve one another.

1 PETER 4:10

WHEN YOU NEED TO BE REMINDED OF THE IMPORTANCE OF PROVIDING FOR YOUR FAMILY . . .

Those who won't care for their relatives, especially those in their own household, have denied the true faith. Such people are worse than unbelievers.

1 TIMOTHY 5:8

WHEN YOU NEED TO HEAR THAT GOD IS WATCHING OVER GODLY FAMILIES . . .

He will bless those who fear the LORD,
    both great and lowly.
May the LORD richly bless
    both you and your children.

PSALM 115:13-14

Fear ⟶

My childhood was less than idyllic. The details aren't important, but the legacy it left behind was fear. I am often afraid for no obvious reason. I may be cooking or writing or praying or riding in the car, and suddenly I find my heart racing in abject fear. Or sometimes I'm afraid for a much more obvious reason. Perhaps my teen was supposed to be home by 11 p.m., and it's now nearly midnight, and they're not home, and they're not answering their phone.

In all my years of struggling with fear, my biggest breakthrough came when a friend pointed out that fear is a spiritual response. Both rational and irrational fear are driven by spiritual forces, and I can either succumb to them or resist them. God's Word carries great power over the spirit of fear. The next time you find yourself doing battle with the spirit of fear, try some of these: speak God's Word, pray, listen to worship music, and declare what you know to be true. It may not happen all at once, this victory over fear. It may not be complete victory the first time, or perhaps anytime. But our victory is always found not in who we are, but in who God is. Recognize fear for what it is: an assault against a daughter of the King. Speak truth, precious mom! Let your children see you praising God in the midst of your struggle. God is by your side. He will help you.

WHEN YOU ARE TEMPTED TO GIVE IN TO A SPIRIT OF FEAR . . .

God has not given us a spirit of fear and timidity, but of power, love, and self-discipline.

2 TIMOTHY 1:7

WHEN YOUR MOTHER'S HEART IS TEMPTED TO PANIC . . .

Be still, and know that I am God!
  I will be honored by every nation.
  I will be honored throughout the world.
  PSALM 46:10

WHEN YOUR FEAR CAUSES YOU TO FORGET ABOUT PRAYER . . .

In my distress I prayed to the LORD,
  and the LORD answered me and set me free.
The LORD is for me, so I will have no fear.
  What can mere people do to me?
  PSALM 118:5-6

**WHEN YOUR CHILD NEEDS REASSURANCE
THAT GOD IS THEIR HELPER . . .**

See, God has come to save me.
  I will trust in him and not be afraid.
The LORD GOD is my strength and my song;
  he has given me victory.
  ISAIAH 12:2

Forgiveness

**WHEN IT HELPS TO REMEMBER THAT
GOD STANDS WILLING TO FORGIVE YOU . . .**

He does not punish us for all our sins;
  he does not deal harshly with us, as we deserve.

For his unfailing love toward those who fear him
    is as great as the height of the heavens above the earth.
He has removed our sins as far from us
    as the east is from the west.
    PSALM 103:10-12

LORD, if you kept a record of our sins,
    who, O Lord, could ever survive?
But you offer forgiveness,
    that we might learn to fear you.
    PSALM 130:3-4

WHEN YOU NEED TO MODEL
TRUE FORGIVENESS FOR YOUR CHILDREN . . .

Be kind to each other, tenderhearted, forgiving one
another, just as God through Christ has forgiven you.
    EPHESIANS 4:32

WHEN YOU'RE TEMPTED TO REMAIN ANGRY . . .

"Don't sin by letting anger control you." Don't let the
sun go down while you are still angry, for anger gives a
foothold to the devil.
    EPHESIANS 4:26-27

WHEN UNFORGIVENESS SETTLES INTO
THE SECRET PLACES OF YOUR HEART . . .

When you are praying, first forgive anyone you are
holding a grudge against, so that your Father in heaven
will forgive your sins, too.
    MARK 11:25

Friends ⟶

Over the years Jay and I have developed many friendships. Some were temporary while others continue year after year. We have dear friends that live halfway across the country and within that relationship we've found comrades who have laughed and cried with us, celebrated with us, and comforted us in our times of mourning. The Trinity has existed since the time that was before time: Father, Son, and Holy Spirit have enjoyed some sort of divine friendship that is beyond our understanding. But they have given our hearts the desire for friendship too. We long for relationships where we can be real, honest, and transparent; where we know we'll never find condemnation but rather acceptance and love. The Lord wants you to experience friendship at this level. If you have this kind of friendship in your life, give thanks and guard that friendship like the treasure it is. And if you're not experiencing that right now, ask God to bring a true friend into your life. He answers prayer—and friendships are close to His father's heart.

WHEN YOU SEE OTHER MOTHERS STRUGGLING AND NEEDING A FRIEND . . .

Let us think of ways to motivate one another to acts of love and good works. And let us not neglect our meeting together, as some people do, but encourage one another, especially now that the day of his return is drawing near.

HEBREWS 10:24-25

WHEN YOU NEED TO STRESS THE IMPORTANCE
OF GOOD FRIENDS TO YOUR CHILDREN . . .

Walk with the wise and become wise;
    associate with fools and get in trouble.
    PROVERBS 13:20

There are "friends" who destroy each other,
    but a real friend sticks closer than a brother.
    PROVERBS 18:24

As iron sharpens iron,
    so a friend sharpens a friend.
    PROVERBS 27:17

Future

WHEN YOU NEED TO REMIND YOURSELF (OR YOUR CHILD)
THAT GOD'S PLANS ARE ALWAYS GOOD . . .

"I know the plans I have for you," says the LORD.
"They are plans for good and not for disaster, to give
you a future and a hope."
    JEREMIAH 29:11

WHEN YOU START TO WORRY ABOUT THE FUTURE . . .

So don't worry about these things, saying, "What will
we eat? What will we drink? What will we wear?" These
things dominate the thoughts of unbelievers, but your
heavenly Father already knows all your needs. Seek the
Kingdom of God above all else, and live righteously,

and he will give you everything you need. So don't
worry about tomorrow, for tomorrow will bring its own
worries. Today's trouble is enough for today.

MATTHEW 6:31-34

WHEN YOU NEED TO REMEMBER THAT
YOU'RE JUST PASSING THROUGH . . .

Since you have been raised to new life with Christ, set
your sights on the realities of heaven, where Christ sits
in the place of honor at God's right hand. Think about
the things of heaven, not the things of earth.

COLOSSIANS 3:1-2

WHEN YOU NEED TO PICTURE A GODLY WOMAN
WHO IS UNAFRAID OF THE FUTURE . . .

She is clothed with strength and dignity,
    and she laughs without fear of the future.
When she speaks, her words are wise,
    and she gives instructions with kindness.
She carefully watches everything in her household
    and suffers nothing from laziness.

Her children stand and bless her.
    Her husband praises her:
"There are many virtuous and capable women in the
        world,
    but you surpass them all!"

Charm is deceptive, and beauty does not last;
    but a woman who fears the LORD will be greatly
        praised.

Reward her for all she has done.
    Let her deeds publicly declare her praise.
    PROVERBS 31:25-31

God's Will

**WHEN YOU NEED TO HEAR THAT GOD
HAS A RIGHT PATH FOR YOUR FAMILY ...**

Show me the right path, O LORD;
    point out the road for me to follow.
Lead me by your truth and teach me,
    for you are the God who saves me.
    All day long I put my hope in you. . . .

He leads the humble in doing right,
    teaching them his way.
    PSALM 25:4-5, 9

WHEN YOU NEED TO KNOW WHERE TO GO FOR HELP ...

Your word is a lamp to guide my feet
    and a light for my path.
    PSALM 119:105

WHEN YOU QUESTION IF GOD'S WILL BRINGS JOY ...

The LORD directs the steps of the godly.
    He delights in every detail of their lives.
Though they stumble, they will never fall,
    for the LORD holds them by the hand.
    PSALM 37:23-24

Grace ⟶

A friend once related to me the tale of an old gentleman with a third-grade education who shared a simple but profound truth. This uneducated old man said, "Mercy is when the Lord don't give ya what ya had a-comin', and grace is when he gives ya what ya didn't have a-comin'." These are words so profound that angels might meditate on them, yet so simple that even a child could understand them. Grace is the oil that keeps relationships running smoothly—and grace is what allows us to have a relationship with God at all. There isn't a day that goes by that I don't need to receive the grace of my husband and children. Nor is there a day that I don't need to extend grace to them as well. And more important is my need for God's grace. Paul talked about his determination to live each day in a manner pleasing to God only to discover that he had failed in ways that grieved Him. And yet . . . and yet God's grace is fresh each morning as we experience a new beginning and discover we didn't get what we "had a-comin'." Paul reminds us that we're not to continue in deliberate sin, but I'm so grateful that when life gets the better of me, God's grace is always there to meet me. Give your family grace. Give yourself grace. And thank the Lord for His relentless, overwhelming grace that pursues you again and again.

WHEN YOU THINK IT'S ALL UP TO YOU . . .

We believe that we are all saved the same way, by the undeserved grace of the Lord Jesus.

ACTS 15:11

God saved you by his grace when you believed. And you can't take credit for this; it is a gift from God. Salvation is not a reward for the good things we have done, so none of us can boast about it.

EPHESIANS 2:8-9

WHEN YOUR CHILD NEEDS TO KNOW THAT GRACE IS ALWAYS AVAILABLE . . .

Let us come boldly to the throne of our gracious God. There we will receive his mercy, and we will find grace to help us when we need it most.

HEBREWS 4:16

WHEN YOU'VE REACHED THE END OF YOUR OWN STRENGTH . . .

Each time he said, "My grace is all you need. My power works best in weakness." So now I am glad to boast about my weaknesses, so that the power of Christ can work through me. That's why I take pleasure in my weaknesses, and in the insults, hardships, persecutions, and troubles that I suffer for Christ. For when I am weak, then I am strong.

2 CORINTHIANS 12:9-10

Grief

Grief is real, and it is relentless sometimes. As a pastor's wife, I have witnessed grief as it rips through families and into the hearts of parents—but I never understood how

God works in the deep places of grief until it hit my family through the pain of abandonment. Some years ago I had a close family member who walked away from the Lord and our family simultaneously. Until that day I had never experienced grief like that. I couldn't stop crying, and it felt like my heart was literally breaking when I saw the destruction and pain that were left in the wake of this person's selfish choice. But at the darkest moment of my grief, I remembered that my Savior was familiar with my pain. The Bible tells us that Jesus was a man acquainted with sorrows. He, too, had been betrayed. He, too, had seen the destruction and pain that sin causes. Did knowing that make the pain stop instantly? No, of course not, but I felt His presence more closely after that.

Grief is a part of love. The more intensely we love, the more intensely we experience grief, whether at a failed pregnancy, the stillbirth of a child, the loss of a family member, or the dissolution of a marriage when a spouse simply walks away. But Jesus meets us in our suffering, and in Him we can find fellowship and peace even in the midst of that suffering. I wouldn't want to experience that grief and pain again, but I will be forever grateful for the ways in which the Lord comforted me during that season.

WHEN YOU NEED TO KNOW GOD IS NEAR YOU IN YOUR SUFFERING . . .

The LORD is close to the brokenhearted;
> he rescues those whose spirits are crushed.
>
> PSALM 34:18

WHEN YOU WONDER IF YOU WILL EVER FIND JOY AGAIN . . .

You have sorrow now, but I will see you again; then
you will rejoice, and no one can rob you of that joy.

JOHN 16:22

**WHEN YOU NEED SUPERNATURAL
STRENGTH IN THE MIDST OF GRIEF . . .**

My health may fail, and my spirit may grow weak,
    but God remains the strength of my heart;
    he is mine forever.

PSALM 73:26

WHEN YOUR GRIEF MAKES YOU FEEL FAR AWAY FROM GOD . . .

I am convinced that nothing can ever separate us from
God's love. Neither death nor life, neither angels nor
demons, neither our fears for today nor our worries
about tomorrow—not even the powers of hell can
separate us from God's love. No power in the sky above
or in the earth below—indeed, nothing in all creation
will ever be able to separate us from the love of God
that is revealed in Christ Jesus our Lord.

ROMANS 8:38-39

Guidance

WHEN YOU DON'T KNOW WHAT TO DO . . .

Trust in the LORD with all your heart;
    do not depend on your own understanding.

Seek his will in all you do,
>   and he will show you which path to take.
>   PROVERBS 3:5-6

Happiness ⟶

WHEN YOUR CHILD HAS AN UNHAPPY DISPOSITION . . .

Take delight in the LORD,
>   and he will give you your heart's desires.

Commit everything you do to the LORD.
>   Trust him, and he will help you.
He will make your innocence radiate like the dawn,
>   and the justice of your cause will shine like the
>   noonday sun.

Be still in the presence of the LORD,
>   and wait patiently for him to act.
Don't worry about evil people who prosper
>   or fret about their wicked schemes.
>   PSALM 37:4-7

WHEN YOU LOOK FOR HAPPINESS IN MOTHERING . . .

I decided there is nothing better than to enjoy food
and drink and to find satisfaction in work. Then I
realized that these pleasures are from the hand of God.
For who can eat or enjoy anything apart from him?
God gives wisdom, knowledge, and joy to those who
please him. But if a sinner becomes wealthy, God takes

the wealth away and gives it to those who please him.
This, too, is meaningless—like chasing the wind.

ECCLESIASTES 2:24-26

Healing ⟶

I've never been quite the same since having a profound conversation with a brilliant physician. This man has the credentials and success stories that most doctors can only dream about, but his humble words changed my worldview forever. He said, "I can't heal anyone. I didn't know that as a young doctor fresh out of medical school, but I know it now. I can perform the exact same operation on two individuals with identical diagnoses. One heals beautifully and recovers fully, while the other one languishes and eventually dies. I did nothing different. I don't have the power to make a bone rejoin, an incision grow back together, or a brain begin functioning after surgery. Healing is God's domain." That's right, isn't it? Whether we need healing of the soul or healing of the body, ultimately our trust rests in the Healer. We pursue medication. We consult with physicians. We follow regimens. But in the end, we are dependent on the Lord Jesus. He is Jehovah-Rapha, our healer.

WHEN YOU NEED HEALING . . .

O LORD, if you heal me, I will be truly healed;
    if you save me, I will be truly saved.
    My praises are for you alone!

JEREMIAH 17:14

O LORD my God, I cried to you for help,
  and you restored my health.
  PSALM 30:2

WHEN YOU WONDER HOW POWERFUL YOUR PRAYERS ARE . . .

Confess your sins to each other and pray for each
other so that you may be healed. The earnest prayer
of a righteous person has great power and produces
wonderful results.
  JAMES 5:16

**WHEN YOU STRUGGLE TO HAVE JOY
WHILE YOU WAIT FOR HEALING . . .**

Because you are my helper,
  I sing for joy in the shadow of your wings.
  PSALM 63:7

Heartbreak

Years ago, I sat with a precious friend whose heart was broken. Her husband had run away with a younger woman and all of their money. She was left with their two sons and an empty bank account. This was the man who had pledged to love and cherish her until death parted them. I've never seen anyone sob the way my friend sobbed. We collapsed onto the floor, and I cried with her as she tried to come to terms with this incomprehensible, unjust outcome. This was not the life she had imagined. This world can be so hard, can't it?

I've come to believe that God does His best work in the deep places. When we go through deep water, He is there. We may not know all the answers, but we do know the Healer. Today, my friend is remarried and is living a wonderful life. God is in the business of mending broken hearts. Whether we're experiencing the heartbreak of a prodigal child, a broken marriage, or a friend's betrayal, the Lord is never more than a whisper away, and He is leaning forward from His throne, eager to help us get through the impossible. He is the God of new beginnings.

WHEN YOUR CHILD'S HEART IS BROKEN . . .

The Lord is close to the brokenhearted;
> he rescues those whose spirits are crushed.
> PSALM 34:18

I hold you by your right hand—
> I, the Lord your God.
And I say to you,
> "Don't be afraid. I am here to help you."
> ISAIAH 41:13

WHEN YOU STRUGGLE TO MAKE SENSE OF THE HURT . . .

The Lord hears his people when they call to him
> for help.
> He rescues them from all their troubles.
> PSALM 34:17

We know that God causes everything to work together for the good of those who love God and are called according to his purpose for them.

ROMANS 8:28

Hope

"His situation is hopeless." That's what the doctors told us after my nephew Bobby had been involved in a horrible traffic accident. "His brain is nonresponsive, and people do not recover from these kinds of injuries." I'm sure Lazarus's family thought his situation was hopeless too. But if there's one thing I've learned, it's this: there is always hope with God. We serve a God of hope. Whether it's Lazarus's lifeless body laid in the tomb or my nephew lying comatose in the hospital, no circumstances are too difficult for God. Jesus raised Lazarus from the dead, and God also healed my nephew. If you're facing a "hopeless situation," I urge you to begin to read Scripture. God's Word is a continuous testimony of hope from Genesis to Revelation. Don't side with the enemy and give up the hope that the Lord wants to give you.

WHEN YOU FEEL WORRIED ABOUT HOW THINGS WILL TURN OUT . . .

Prepare your minds for action and exercise self-control. Put all your hope in the gracious salvation that will come to you when Jesus Christ is revealed to the world.

1 PETER 1:13

WHEN THE OUTCOME YOU'RE FACING IS UNCERTAIN . . .

I am certain that God, who began the good work
within you, will continue his work until it is finally
finished on the day when Christ Jesus returns.

PHILIPPIANS 1:6

WHEN YOU NEED TO REMEMBER THE SOURCE OF YOUR HOPE . . .

We put our hope in the LORD.
He is our help and our shield.

PSALM 33:20

I pray that God, the source of hope, will fill you
completely with joy and peace because you trust in
him. Then you will overflow with confident hope
through the power of the Holy Spirit.

ROMANS 15:13

Hospitality ⟶

The Pharisees were scandalized when Jesus sat and ate with
sinners. They understood that breaking bread together is the
ultimate expression of friendship and intimacy. We are com-
manded to be hospitable to others, even as God has invited us
to sit at His table. But here's the thing. We live in a world poi-
soned by Pinterest and fractured by Facebook. We've believed
the lie that hospitality has to look like Martha Stewart and our
cooking has to match the Pioneer Woman. It's a lie from the
enemy who wants us to feel inadequate and incapable. Whether

our hospitality is represented by a five-course meal and a private guesthouse next to the pool or a warm bowl of soup from the Instant Pot and a hide-a-bed sofa, it's just as much an expression of hospitality to our guest. Don't let the paralysis of perfectionism keep you from inviting people into your home and into your life. Share generously of what you have and love the people God places in your path. There's a blessing in it!

WHEN YOU HAVE A CHANCE TO OPEN YOUR HOME TO OTHERS . . .

Most important of all, continue to show deep love for each other, for love covers a multitude of sins. Cheerfully share your home with those who need a meal or a place to stay.

1 PETER 4:8-9

God has given each of you a gift from his great variety of spiritual gifts. Use them well to serve one another.

1 PETER 4:10

Infertility

Few words strike more fear into the heart of a woman than the word *infertile*. Over the past thirty years, I've sat and cried with many women who have struggled to conceive. It's devastating— and for many couples, what hurts the most is the reality that the life they're living is not going to look like the one they had planned. We like to think we're in control. We have our reminder apps on our smartphones and our beautifully illustrated daily planners complete with inspirational sayings. But in the end there are some things we can't plan for. There are some things that we cannot control, including our ability to conceive a child. And while there are no simple words of consolation for the woman who longs to have a child of her own, there is hope. Our hope is found in the knowledge that even when things feel beyond our control, God's plans for us are good. He cares. Let Him comfort you. Run to Him. Fall into His arms—and trust Him. His heart toward you is good.

WHEN YOUR ARMS ACHE FOR A CHILD . . .

I am counting on the LORD;
> yes, I am counting on him.
> I have put my hope in his word.
> PSALM 130:5

Rejoice in our confident hope. Be patient in trouble, and keep on praying.
> ROMANS 12:12

WHEN YOUR PRAYERS FOR A CHILD HAVE BEEN ANSWERED . . .

He gives the childless woman a family,
> making her a happy mother.

Praise the LORD!
> PSALM 113:9

WHEN YOU NEED TO HEAR THAT GOD CAN DO ANYTHING . . .

Isaac pleaded with the LORD on behalf of his wife, because she was unable to have children. The LORD answered Isaac's prayer, and Rebekah became pregnant with twins.

GENESIS 25:21

It was by faith that even Sarah was able to have a child, though she was barren and was too old. She believed that God would keep his promise.

HEBREWS 11:11

WHEN YOUR LONGING CAUSES YOU TO DOUBT GOD'S HEART . . .

The LORD God is our sun and our shield.
    He gives us grace and glory.
The LORD will withhold no good thing
    from those who do what is right.

PSALM 84:11

Injustice ⁓

WHEN YOU FEEL THAT GOD IS UNJUST . . .

The LORD is still there in the city,
    and he does no wrong.
Day by day he hands down justice,
    and he does not fail.
    But the wicked know no shame.

ZEPHANIAH 3:5

Are we saying, then, that God was unfair? Of course not!

ROMANS 9:14

In my distress I prayed to the LORD,
  and the LORD answered me and set me free.
The LORD is for me, so I will have no fear.
  What can mere people do to me?
PSALM 118:5-6

Insecurity

I am a speaker by profession—but I have a confession to make. I rarely climb those platform steps as I'm being introduced without feeling insecure. The relentless, nagging, destructive voice of the enemy is always whispering as I climb each step, "You're not good enough, they're going to hate you, you didn't prepare well enough, you won't be as good as _____." We all hear that voice, don't we? Sometimes it's over our parenting, our homemaking, or even our cooking! (Ask me how I know.) No matter the reason, the tactic is clear: the devil wants to wear us down. The devil wants us to compare ourselves to others because he knows that comparison is the thief of contentment. Stand firm. Your worth comes from the One in whom we find our ultimate security. His name is Jesus. Never allow the accuser to define your worth or position. You are what God says you are: loved, chosen, redeemed.

Oh, don't worry; we wouldn't dare say that we are as wonderful as these [others] who tell you how important they are! But they are only comparing themselves with each other, using themselves as the standard of measurement. How ignorant!

2 CORINTHIANS 10:12

WHEN INSECURITY CLOUDS YOUR THINKING . . .

I know how to live on almost nothing or with everything. I have learned the secret of living in every situation, whether it is with a full stomach or empty, with plenty or little. For I can do everything through Christ, who gives me strength.

PHILIPPIANS 4:12-13

Integrity

WHEN YOU ARE GIVEN A CHANCE TO CHOOSE . . .

If you refuse to serve the LORD, then choose today whom you will serve. Would you prefer the gods your ancestors served beyond the Euphrates? Or will it be the gods of the Amorites in whose land you now live? But as for me and my family, we will serve the LORD.

JOSHUA 24:15

**WHEN YOUR CHILDREN NEED
TO LEARN WHY INTEGRITY MATTERS . . .**

Follow the steps of the good,
    and stay on the paths of the righteous.
For only the godly will live in the land,
    and those with integrity will remain in it.
    PROVERBS 2:20-21

WHEN YOU WONDER IF GOD CARES ABOUT YOUR DECISIONS . . .

The godly walk with integrity;
    blessed are their children who follow them. . . .

Even children are known by the way they act,
    whether their conduct is pure, and whether it is
        right.
    PROVERBS 20:7, 11

The blameless will be rescued from harm,
    but the crooked will be suddenly destroyed.
    PROVERBS 28:18

Joy

Do you believe that joy is dependent on your circumstances? Even though I may not believe that, I can tell you, I've sure acted like it's true. I've experienced disappointment, discouragement, and betrayal. I've looked at the bill pile and then at the checkbook. I've looked at the broken washing machine and the six laundry baskets stacked nearby. Satan loves to make sure we're living with a victim mentality. In fact, he is hoping that we'll shake our fist and curse God. He's hoping that our current challenges will cause us to doubt God's goodness. When you're struggling to have a good attitude, remember this: joy is a fruit of the Spirit. It's evidence of God's work in our lives, and it has nothing at all to do with our circumstances. Another by-product of joy is a changed attitude—and don't moms want that for their children? Remember, we can't give our kids what we don't have. We can give in to our emotions, or we can choose our response. Let's choose joy, moms! And let's pray that our children learn to choose joy too. It starts with our example!

WHEN YOU NEED A REASON TO REJOICE . . .

I will be glad and rejoice in your unfailing love,
>   for you have seen my troubles,
>   and you care about the anguish of my soul.
>   PSALM 31:7

Songs of joy and victory are sung in the camp of the
>   godly.
>   The strong right arm of the LORD has done
>   glorious things!
>   PSALM 118:15

legacy

How often do we think of our legacy? My hunch is that, like me, you're more worried about what you're going to make for dinner right now than you are about leaving a legacy for your children—but Scripture teaches that we should live with our legacy in mind. Death isn't a question of if, but rather of when. When the funeral is over and the mourners have gone their separate ways, the thing that will remain is our legacy. Our legacy in death is a function of the choices we make in life. The word *character* derives from a Greek word meaning "emboss" or "engrave." As we make consistent choices over time, they leave a permanent mark on our character. We become what we choose, and the legacy we leave is a function of the choices we've made day by day. What choices are you making right now? How will they impact the legacy you leave behind? What will your life say about who and what you choose to love? By God's grace, we can leave behind a legacy of love that will be passed on for generations.

WHEN YOU WONDER HOW LONG GOD'S FAITHFULNESS WILL LAST . . .

The LORD is good.
> His unfailing love continues forever,
> and his faithfulness continues to each generation.
PSALM 100:5

WHEN YOU NEED THE EXAMPLE OF A FAITHFUL MOTHER . . .

I remember your genuine faith, for you share the faith that first filled your grandmother Lois and your mother, Eunice. And I know that same faith continues strong in you.
2 TIMOTHY 1:5

WHEN YOU WONDER IF YOUR INFLUENCE MATTERS . . .

Older women likewise are to be reverent in behavior, not slanderers or slaves to much wine. They are to teach what is good, and so train the young women to love their husbands and children, to be self-controlled, pure, working at home, kind, and submissive to their own husbands, that the word of God may not be reviled.

TITUS 2:3-5, ESV

WHEN YOU THINK OF THE BLESSING OF SEEING YOUR GRANDCHILDREN . . .

How joyful are those who fear the LORD—
    all who follow his ways!
You will enjoy the fruit of your labor.
    How joyful and prosperous you will be! . . .

May the LORD continually bless you from Zion.
    May you see Jerusalem prosper as long as you live.
May you live to enjoy your grandchildren.
    May Israel have peace!

PSALM 128:1-2, 5-6

loss

Loss comes in many forms, doesn't it? Maybe you've experienced a miscarriage. Maybe you've had a home foreclosed on or experienced the betrayal of a friend or been cheated in an

unscrupulous business deal. Loss is a part of living. We mourn
and grieve when we experience loss. And we should. But we
who claim the name of Christ have a hope that goes beyond
a temporal loss. We worship the One who is Justice and is the
Restorer. Near the very end of the Bible the Lord says, "Look, I
am making everything new!" (Revelation 21:5). Did you catch
that, mom? Read that verse again and let it sink in. Everything.
New. All that we've ever lost will be restored to us someday.
Every injustice will be made right. All that's been stolen will be
given back. All that we willingly lost for the sake of the gospel will
be returned to us. God is in the business of restoring that which
was lost . . . including us. We who were once lost and separated
from the Lord have been found and given new life. When we
experience loss, we need to remember that our children are
watching how we process it. Are we pointing them to Jesus? Or
are we making them bitter toward the God who loves them?
We don't get to determine the losses we suffer, but we do get to
choose how we respond to that suffering.

WHEN YOU NEED TO BE ENCOURAGED THAT GOD CAN RESTORE WHAT YOU HAVE LOST . . .

When Job prayed for his friends, the LORD restored
his fortunes. In fact, the LORD gave him twice as much
as before!

JOB 42:10

The LORD says, "I will give you back what you lost
    to the swarming locusts, the hopping locusts,
the stripping locusts, and the cutting locusts."

JOEL 2:25

[The LORD says,] "I will comfort you there in
    Jerusalem
    as a mother comforts her child."
ISAIAH 66:13

Love

When our youngest was seven, she broke her arm in spec-
tacular fashion. Naturally, we were in the other room when
she fell. She assured us she had been chasing a balloon and
tripped, landing awkwardly on her arm. She was in tears,
and we comforted her on the way to the emergency room
where they set her arm and put on a cast. Only when we
got home did she dissolve into tears that were far more
intense than the tears caused by the pain of her injury.
These were tears of guilt as the confession poured out,
words tumbling one over another.

As it turned out, our daughter had not been chasing a balloon when she fell. She had been standing on the coffee table—
something she had been asked repeatedly not to do. And then
for reasons that only she knew, she decided to try a cartwheel
off the forbidden table. Her confession complete, she lay against
my chest waiting for our response. I think she was sure she was
in trouble because of her disobedience and the lie that accom-
panied it. Instead, we held her close and comforted her. She had
learned her lesson the hard way—like many of us do. Surely God

often looks down at us, after we confess that we are suffering from our own poor choices, and says, "Here. Lay your head on My chest. You're forgiven."

God loves us even more than we love our children, even when we are sinful. When we confess our sins and repent from our disobedience, he is quick to forgive. Nothing can ever separate us from the love of God. Nothing.

WHEN YOU NEED A REMINDER OF WHAT LOVE LOOKS LIKE . . .

Love is patient and kind. Love is not jealous or boastful or proud or rude. It does not demand its own way. It is not irritable, and it keeps no record of being wronged. It does not rejoice about injustice but rejoices whenever the truth wins out. Love never gives up, never loses faith, is always hopeful, and endures through every circumstance.

1 CORINTHIANS 13:4-7

WHEN YOU DOUBT THE LOVE OF GOD . . .

This is how God loved the world: He gave his one and only Son, so that everyone who believes in him will not perish but have eternal life. God sent his Son into the world not to judge the world, but to save the world through him.

JOHN 3:16-17

[Jesus said,] "I have loved you even as the Father has loved me."

JOHN 15:9

WHEN YOU NEED TO TEACH YOUR CHILDREN WHERE TRUE LOVE IS FOUND . . .

I am convinced that nothing can ever separate us from God's love. Neither death nor life, neither angels nor demons, neither our fears for today nor our worries about tomorrow—not even the powers of hell can separate us from God's love. No power in the sky above or in the earth below—indeed, nothing in all creation will ever be able to separate us from the love of God that is revealed in Christ Jesus our Lord.

ROMANS 8:38-39

We love each other because he loved us first.

1 JOHN 4:19

WHEN YOU WONDER HOW LONG GOD WILL LOVE YOU . . .

Give thanks to the LORD, for he is good!
    His faithful love endures forever.
Give thanks to the God of gods.
    His faithful love endures forever.
Give thanks to the Lord of lords.
    His faithful love endures forever.

PSALM 136:1-3

WHEN YOUR MOTHER'S HEART THINKS OF THE NEXT GENERATION . . .

The LORD is good.
    His unfailing love continues forever,
    and his faithfulness continues to each generation.

PSALM 100:5

Marriage

I was talking to a friend one day, and he was telling me that from the age of eighteen to thirty-six he smoked. When he quit, it wasn't because of health warnings on the cigarette pack. It was because he didn't want his children to be harmed by secondhand smoke. In other words, what he wouldn't do for himself, he did for love. God calls a man and a woman to join together and become one flesh. And it's within the miracle of that one-flesh relationship that we discover what we're willing to do for love. We discover that we're willing to make sacrifices, to forgive, and to pursue someone else's interests beyond our own. Just as the Holy Trinity is a mystery, so too is marriage. Within that mystery I give and receive mercy and forgiveness, I nurture and I, too, am nurtured, and I earnestly pray for God's best for someone other than myself. I do these things because when one of us prospers, we both prosper. No matter what life is throwing at you today, make time to nurture your marriage. You will likely find that in the end, everything you invest in blessing your husband will come back to bless you as well.

WHEN YOU'RE TEMPTED TO OVERCOMPLICATE WHAT MAKES MARRIAGE WORK . . .

Most important of all, continue to show deep love for each other, for love covers a multitude of sins.

1 PETER 4:8

The man and his wife were both naked, but they felt
no shame.

GENESIS 2:25

**WHEN YOU NEED TO REMEMBER YOU
SERVE YOUR SPOUSE FOR HIS SAKE . . .**

Submit to one another out of reverence for Christ.

EPHESIANS 5:21

Mentoring

I will never forget the first time I meditated on these words
of Jesus in Luke 6:40: "The student who is fully trained will
become like the teacher." Those words sent chills down my spine
as I pondered the reality that my children and grandchildren
are being formed into my likeness as I teach and mentor them.
Whether it's a younger woman God has placed in our lives for
mentoring, or our own children or grandchildren, we have an
amazing opportunity. We can help form their character, their
values, and their habits by the ways in which we mentor them.
There can be no greater privilege than to mentor and shape
the hearts of those God entrusts to our care. Is there a young
woman in your life who needs a mentor? Maybe God is asking
you to invite her into your life. Not sure? Ask Him. He is listening!

WHEN YOU THINK YOUR EXAMPLE DOESN'T MATTER . . .

The student who is fully trained will become like the teacher.
LUKE 6:40

I urge you to imitate me.
1 CORINTHIANS 4:16

WHEN YOU NEED ENCOURAGEMENT TO FOLLOW GODLY PEOPLE AS YOU GROW IN YOUR WALK WITH GOD . . .

You should imitate me, just as I imitate Christ.
1 CORINTHIANS 11:1

Dear brothers and sisters, pattern your lives after mine, and learn from those who follow our example.
PHILIPPIANS 3:17

WHEN YOU FORGET THAT YOUR CHILDREN ARE WATCHING . . .

Keep putting into practice all you learned and received from me—everything you heard from me and saw me doing. Then the God of peace will be with you.
PHILIPPIANS 4:9

WHEN YOUR LACK OF CREDENTIALS KEEPS YOU FROM WALKING IN POWER . . .

Don't let anyone think less of you because you are young. Be an example to all believers in what you say, in the way you live, in your love, your faith, and your purity.
1 TIMOTHY 4:12

Mercy ⟶

My husband was still snoring softly as the darkness faded into light. I rubbed my eyes and looked around our bedroom. I sat up slowly in bed, remembering the harsh words I had spoken to my son less than eight hours before when I reminded him for the third time that he was supposed to be studying his algebra instead of talking on his phone. I regretted that my words had betrayed my frustration. But as I flipped open my Bible, my eyes fell on these words in Lamentations 3:22-23: "His mercies never come to an end; they are new every morning" (ESV). Before the sun had even risen, I chose to accept God's mercy. I can forgive myself for harsh words spoken, and I can extend that same mercy to those around me who may not make the best choices today. The Latin word *merces* means "the price paid for something." Jesus paid the price. I am free to accept or reject His mercy in my life today. Strong moms humbly accept God's mercy and in turn extend it freely to others. We serve the God of mercy. The price has been paid.

WHEN YOU WANT YOUR CHILDREN TO UNDERSTAND MERCY . . .

Now go and learn the meaning of this Scripture: "I want you to show mercy, not offer sacrifices." For I have come to call not those who think they are righteous, but those who know they are sinners.

MATTHEW 9:13

Let us come boldly to the throne of our gracious God.
There we will receive his mercy, and we will find grace
to help us when we need it most.

HEBREWS 4:16

Miscarriage

The Bible tells the extraordinary story of God's watching His only
Son die on the cross. God is well acquainted with the sorrow of
losing a child, and He is near to those who are brokenhearted.
I felt His nearness when I suffered a miscarriage after our third
child. My heart ached as I waited to hear our baby's heartbeat
one more time—but there was nothing. It took some time, but
together, Jay and I grieved the loss of our precious little one. The
pain of miscarriage is real, but so is the healing power of Jesus. As
our family grieved our loss, the nearness of God became more
real to me than it had ever been. This is the heart of our Savior—
he weeps when we weep.

Even young people can intuitively understand the heartbreak of a miscarriage through the simple act of watching someone fold up dreams and place them in a box. A friend's daughter
was a theater major, and one of her assignments in college was
to write and perform an original monologue for her class. She
chose to play the role of a young woman who had experienced
a miscarriage. As she spoke about her broken dreams, she

carefully and meticulously folded up a pile of newborn baby clothes, gently placing them in a cardboard box and taping it shut. There wasn't a dry eye in the room.

Thank God we have someone to go to who is familiar with the grief of losing a child. Whether you are in pain right now, or you are carrying a friend to the feet of the Healer, be encouraged. In Him we find comfort and hope. He understands our sorrow.

WHEN YOUR BROKEN MOTHER-HEART IS DESPERATE TO KNOW HE CARES . . .

The LORD is close to the brokenhearted;
> he rescues those whose spirits are crushed.
>
> PSALM 34:18

You keep track of all my sorrows.
> You have collected all my tears in your bottle.
> You have recorded each one in your book.
>
> PSALM 56:8

WHEN YOU NEED PEACE . . .

I have told you all this so that you may have peace in me. Here on earth you will have many trials and sorrows. But take heart, because I have overcome the world.

> JOHN 16:33

WHEN YOU'RE READY TO TALK ABOUT IT . . .

Each time he said, "My grace is all you need. My power works best in weakness." So now I am glad to boast about my weaknesses, so that the power of Christ

can work through me. That's why I take pleasure
in my weaknesses, and in the insults, hardships,
persecutions, and troubles that I suffer for Christ.
For when I am weak, then I am strong.

2 CORINTHIANS 12:9-10

WHEN IT'S TIME TO SAY "I TRUST YOU STILL" . . .

The LORD gave me what I had,
and the LORD has taken it away.
Praise the name of the LORD!

JOB 1:21

Motherhood

As I write this I'm sitting in the cove off the corner of my
bedroom. My husband is downstairs working on a project,
and I've just been interrupted a dozen times in the last half
hour by children coming in to ask questions. Has there
ever been a job more daunting than motherhood? It's a
never-ending job that can easily consume our every wak-
ing moment. I remember a time when I was pregnant with
our first child and I didn't think I'd be a very good mother.
I remember thinking that if I were God I would choose
someone else to raise the precious baby He had chosen
just for me. But I was wrong. God chooses to partner with
us in raising the next generation. It's a powerful truth,
isn't it? He is up before we are, and He's awake all night,

watching over us and our children as our weary bodies recharge with much-needed rest. We have no greater job, no more awesome responsibility, and no more rewarding opportunity than to shape the hearts and minds of our children as we introduce them to the One who created them, died for them, and loves them with a fierceness that even we can't understand. Stay in there for your kids, sweet mom. What you are doing matters more than you may ever know.

WHEN YOU NEED TO HEAR "YOUR KIDS ARE WORTH IT!" . . .

Children are a gift from the LORD;
    they are a reward from him.
    PSALM 127:3

Anyone who welcomes a little child like this on my behalf welcomes me, and anyone who welcomes me welcomes not only me but also my Father who sent me.
    MARK 9:37

WHEN YOUR MOTHER'S HEART IS WEARY . . .

She is clothed with strength and dignity,
    and she laughs without fear of the future.
When she speaks, her words are wise,
    and she gives instructions with kindness.
She carefully watches everything in her household
    and suffers nothing from laziness.

Her children stand and bless her.
    Her husband praises her:

"There are many virtuous and capable women in
       the world,
   but you surpass them all!"

Charm is deceptive, and beauty does not last;
   but a woman who fears the LORD will be greatly
       praised.
PROVERBS 31:25-30

Obedience ⟶

**WHEN YOU WANT TO SHARE THE BLESSING
OF OBEDIENCE WITH YOUR CHILDREN . . .**

How joyful are those who fear the LORD—
   all who follow his ways!
You will enjoy the fruit of your labor.
   How joyful and prosperous you will be!
PSALM 128:1-2

WHEN YOUR HEART NEEDS TO LINE UP WITH GOD'S HEART . . .

Look, today I am giving you the choice between a
blessing and a curse! You will be blessed if you obey
the commands of the LORD your God that I am
giving you today. But you will be cursed if you reject
the commands of the LORD your God and turn away
from him and worship gods you have not known
before.

DEUTERONOMY 11:26-28

WHEN OBEDIENCE FEELS TOO HARD . . .

Samuel replied,

"What is more pleasing to the LORD:
    your burnt offerings and sacrifices
    or your obedience to his voice?
Listen! Obedience is better than sacrifice,
    and submission is better than offering the fat of rams.
Rebellion is as sinful as witchcraft,
    and stubbornness as bad as worshiping idols.
So because you have rejected the command of the LORD,
    he has rejected you as king."

    1 SAMUEL 15:22-23

**WHEN YOU'RE TEMPTED TO GIVE
LIP SERVICE INSTEAD OF OBEDIENCE . . .**

Don't just listen to God's word. You must do what it says. Otherwise, you are only fooling yourselves.

    JAMES 1:22

Opportunity

**WHEN YOU WONDER IF THIS IS THE
OPEN DOOR YOU'VE BEEN ASKING FOR . . .**

We are confident that he hears us whenever we ask for anything that pleases him. And since we know he hears us when we make our requests, we also know that he will give us what we ask for.

    1 JOHN 5:14-15

**WHEN YOU NEED TO REMEMBER THAT
THERE'S A RIGHT TIME FOR EVERYTHING . . .**

For everything there is a season,
a time for every activity under heaven.
A time to be born and a time to die.
A time to plant and a time to harvest.
ECCLESIASTES 3:1-2

WHEN YOU DOUBT GOD'S HEART TOWARD YOU . . .

The LORD God is our sun and our shield.
He gives us grace and glory.
The LORD will withhold no good thing
from those who do what is right.
PSALM 84:11

Overwhelmed

Have you ever felt like you were going under again and
again, submerged beneath the endless responsibilities of
a mother's life? I have. To be *overwhelmed* means literally
to be "thrown over, turned upside down and submerged
completely." Can you relate, mom? We can be overwhelmed by our fears, our responsibilities, or the uncertainty of the future. But my God promises He will not give
me more than I can bear. He promises that, like Peter, I can
choose to keep my eyes on Him and rise above my circumstances and walk on the water that seeks to submerge me.

Whenever I put my eyes on myself or my to-do list or my calendar or my checkbook, I can begin to go under. Look up, mom! Look up to the One who calls us to be overcomers. Like our children, we get to choose: we can be overwhelmed by life or be an overcomer. It all comes down to where we look.

WHEN YOU AND YOUR CHILDREN
NEED A DRINK OF LIVING WATER . . .

O God, you are my God;
    I earnestly search for you.
My soul thirsts for you;
    my whole body longs for you
in this parched and weary land
    where there is no water.
    PSALM 63:1

WHEN YOU'RE OVERWHELMED BY FEAR . . .

In my distress I prayed to the LORD,
    and the LORD answered me and set me free.
The LORD is for me, so I will have no fear.
    What can mere people do to me?
    PSALM 118:5-6

WHEN YOU NEED TO TURN TO GOD DAILY . . .

Praise the Lord; praise God our savior!
    For each day he carries us in his arms.
    PSALM 68:19

We know that God causes everything to work together for the good of those who love God and are called according to his purpose for them.

ROMANS 8:28

Parenting ~

There are a few things in life that I feel pretty good at. I love to write, organize things, and speak. I can cook a mean bowl of soup, and I keep a reasonably clean house. But there is one task that brings me to my knees more quickly than any other: parenting. I don't know about you, mom, but nothing has made me more aware of my need for God's wisdom than the daily challenges of parenting. Have you ever had that one child who manages to stomp on your last nerve every single day? What about the child who simply insists on learning every life lesson the hard way? I realized about a week after my daughter Savannah was born that raising her was something I couldn't do alone. I wasn't equipped. I needed help. I needed divine wisdom, patience, and perspective. Do you need help too? God stands at the ready. God's Word is the only parenting manual you'll ever truly need. Go to Him daily for wisdom. As you study God's Word and lay out the day's agenda in prayer, He will give you strength, and He will partner with you and your husband as you raise the children He has entrusted to your care.

WHEN YOUR CHILD NEEDS TO HEAR THE TRUTH . . .

We will speak the truth in love, growing in every way more and more like Christ, who is the head of his body, the church.

EPHESIANS 4:15

WHEN YOU'RE TEMPTED TO LASH OUT AT YOUR CHILDREN . . .

Gentle words are a tree of life;
    a deceitful tongue crushes the spirit.

PROVERBS 15:4

WHEN YOU REALIZE THE WORLD'S PARENTING WISDOM WON'T SUFFICE . . .

If you need wisdom, ask our generous God, and he will give it to you. He will not rebuke you for asking.

JAMES 1:5

WHEN YOU NEED TO PICK UP YOUR SWORD AND STAY ON THE BATTLEFIELD . . .

We are human, but we don't wage war as humans do. We use God's mighty weapons, not worldly weapons, to knock down the strongholds of human reasoning and to destroy false arguments. We destroy every proud obstacle that keeps people from knowing God. We capture their rebellious thoughts and teach them to obey Christ.

2 CORINTHIANS 10:3-5

Patience

WHEN YOUR CHILDREN ARE BEING DIFFICULT . . .

Love is patient and kind.

1 CORINTHIANS 13:4

Be patient with each other, making allowance for each other's faults because of your love.

EPHESIANS 4:2

WHEN YOUR VIEW NEEDS TO INCLUDE ETERNITY . . .

Jesus replied, "You don't understand now what I am doing, but someday you will."

JOHN 13:7

WHEN YOUR HEART NEEDS A
REASON TO STAND FIRM IN TRIALS . . .

You, too, must be patient. Take courage, for the coming of the Lord is near.

JAMES 5:8

Peace

My father-in-law was a dear man. We all lived in the same big, rambling house together with him and his wife. One night he began experiencing a health crisis. Soon there was an ambulance parked in our driveway and paramedics rushing in with a gurney. My in-laws' living room was a scene of utter chaos with grandchildren crying and my husband and his mother asking questions and paramedics trying to make vital decisions while others prayed quietly, unsure of what to do. The chaos became more intense as we all realized the problem was even more serious than we had thought. And yet . . . in the midst of that storm there was a peace that surpassed all understanding. We didn't know that my precious father-in-law would soon be with the Lord, but we knew that somehow it was going to be all right. The kind of peace we felt in that difficult time is also available to you today. We serve the Prince of Peace, and He stands ready and willing to help us experience peace in the midst of chaos and hope in the midst of despair. He truly does offer peace that passes our human understanding. If you're struggling to find peace today, look to Jesus. His peace is the promise that's offered to every child of God.

WHEN THE WORLD'S PEACE LEAVES YOU UNSATISFIED . . .

I am leaving you with a gift—peace of mind and heart. And the peace I give is a gift the world cannot give. So don't be troubled or afraid.

JOHN 14:27

WHEN YOU WONDER WHERE YOUR PEACE IS COMING FROM . . .

You will experience God's peace, which exceeds anything we can understand. His peace will guard your hearts and minds as you live in Christ Jesus.

PHILIPPIANS 4:7

WHEN PEACE SEEMS TO ELUDE YOU . . .

[Jesus said,] "I have told you all this so that you may have peace in me. Here on earth you will have many trials and sorrows. But take heart, because I have overcome the world."

JOHN 16:33

WHEN YOUR CHILDREN NEED GOD'S PERSPECTIVE ON LIVING AT PEACE WITH OTHERS . . .

Salt is good for seasoning. But if it loses its flavor, how do you make it salty again? You must have the qualities of salt among yourselves and live in peace with each other.

MARK 9:50

Those who are peacemakers will plant seeds of peace and reap a harvest of righteousness.

JAMES 3:18

Perseverance

WHEN YOU FEEL DISQUALIFIED BY YOUR WEAKNESS . . .

Each time he said, "My grace is all you need. My power works best in weakness." So now I am glad to boast about my weaknesses, so that the power of Christ can work through me. That's why I take pleasure in my weaknesses, and in the insults, hardships, persecutions, and troubles that I suffer for Christ. For when I am weak, then I am strong.

2 CORINTHIANS 12:9-10

The righteous person faces many troubles,
    but the LORD comes to the rescue each time.
    PSALM 34:19

He gives power to the weak
    and strength to the powerless.
    ISAIAH 40:29

WHEN YOU NEED ENCOURAGEMENT TO PERSEVERE . . .

I am certain that God, who began the good work
within you, will continue his work until it is finally
finished on the day when Christ Jesus returns.
    PHILIPPIANS 1:6

God blesses those who patiently endure testing and
temptation. Afterward they will receive the crown
of life that God has promised to those who love
him.
    JAMES 1:12

Prayer

There was a time when I was awkward in my prayers, feeling
either self-conscious about my childlike words or stilted because
of my stiff, formal words. And then my second daughter was
born. She never stopped talking, even as an infant. Her bab-
bling and bubbling and cooing didn't communicate any brilliant
ideas or articulate any deep needs. Yet I delighted in holding her

in my lap and listening intently to every sound she made. We were communicating, and I was delighted by her eagerness to talk to me even in the absence of a large vocabulary. We serve a God who invites us to talk with Him. It's not just a monologue, although that's okay too. But it's also a dialogue where He speaks to our heart in ways that surpass language. He is delighted when I want to crawl on His lap and spend time in His presence. On any given day I may or may not have the words, but I bring everything to Him in prayer. I'm not there to demand that He meet my needs. Rather I'm there because I need someone to talk to, and I know He enjoys our exchanges. No matter what situation you face today, mom, take time to sit and talk it over with the God who never slumbers and who is always leaning forward from His throne, eager to spend time with you.

WHEN YOU WONDER IF THOSE
SMALL REQUESTS MATTER TO GOD . . .

Don't worry about anything; instead, pray about everything. Tell God what you need, and thank him for all he has done. Then you will experience God's peace, which exceeds anything we can understand. His peace will guard your hearts and minds as you live in Christ Jesus.

PHILIPPIANS 4:6-7

WHEN YOU DOUBT THE POWER OF PRAYER . . .

I tell you, you can pray for anything, and if you believe that you've received it, it will be yours.

MARK 11:24

We are confident that he hears us whenever we ask for
anything that pleases him. And since we know he hears
us when we make our requests, we also know that he
will give us what we ask for.

1 JOHN 5:14-15

WHEN YOU FEEL LIKE PRAYER ISN'T WORKING . . .

Always be joyful. Never stop praying. Be thankful in
all circumstances, for this is God's will for you who
belong to Christ Jesus.

1 THESSALONIANS 5:16-18

WHEN PRAYER IS ALL YOU HAVE . . .

Confess your sins to each other and pray for each
other so that you may be healed. The earnest prayer
of a righteous person has great power and produces
wonderful results.

JAMES 5:16

WHEN YOU WANT TO LEARN FROM JESUS' PRAYER . . .

Our Father in heaven,
    may your name be kept holy.
May your Kingdom come soon.
May your will be done on earth,
    as it is in heaven.
Give us today the food we need,
and forgive us our sins,
    as we have forgiven those who sin
        against us.

And don't let us yield to temptation,
    but rescue us from the evil one.
MATTHEW 6:9-13

Priorities

"Seek first the kingdom of God and his righteousness"
(Matthew 6:33, ESV). These nine words are so simple, yet they
take a lifetime to master, because the tyranny of the urgent is
always seeking to scramble our priorities. I love the words of
the German writer Goethe who said, "Things which matter
most must never be at the mercy of things which matter least."
That sums it up nicely, doesn't it? While the temptation is to
focus on knowledge instead of character in raising our children, we know that in the end, it's character that matters most.
I have more days than I care to admit when my daily planner
has twenty hours of activities penciled into twelve available
hours. It's on these days especially that I need to prioritize time
with God. By reading His Word and spending time in prayer,
I affirm my priorities as His daughter. Reread the story of the
sisters Martha and Mary found in Luke 10. Martha was so very,
very busy that she missed the opportunity to be with Jesus. Are
you a Martha, or are you a Mary? If we don't get our priorities right, our life will simply be a series of frantic, last-minute
choices rather than the result of a devoted life of divine priorities. Busy mom . . . purpose to spend time with God today and
ask Him to help prioritize your day.

If a man cannot manage his own household, how can
he take care of God's church?

1 TIMOTHY 3:5

Those who won't care for their relatives, especially
those in their own household, have denied the true
faith. Such people are worse than unbelievers.

1 TIMOTHY 5:8

**WHEN YOU NEED TO TEACH YOUR CHILDREN
THAT PLEASING GOD IS OUR FIRST PRIORITY . . .**

Don't copy the behavior and customs of this world,
but let God transform you into a new person by
changing the way you think. Then you will learn
to know God's will for you, which is good and
pleasing and perfect.

ROMANS 12:2

WHEN YOU NEED TO ASSESS WHERE YOUR HEART IS . . .

Where your treasure is, there will your heart be also.

LUKE 12:34, ESV

Prodigals

A friend once said that each child has to go through the
revolving door of salvation. No matter how often a child

attends Sunday school or how much Scripture they memorize or when they are baptized, each one has to enter into a relationship with God on His terms. Some of us catch only a whiff of the world before coming back through that revolving door. But others of us wander in the wilderness for years.

Few things are harder for a mother to deal with than a prodigal child. We've done our part. Now they need to do their part. But no matter how far they wander and no matter what they are doing, they are never alone. Even if we haven't heard from them in years, God is right there with them, gently nudging them toward home. If you are struggling with the pain of watching a child wander from God, don't give up—and don't let your child's decision to walk away from God take you off the battlefield. Your story, when it's given to the Father, will yield a harvest that you cannot imagine. Keep walking with God. Keep praying. Rest in God's provision and lean hard on His love—it endures forever. Pray always, believe always, hope always. He is watching over your child even now.

WHEN MOTHERHOOD HAS LEFT YOU WOUNDED . . .

Bless those who persecute you. Don't curse them; pray that God will bless them. Be happy with those who are happy, and weep with those who weep. Live in harmony with each other. Don't be too proud to enjoy the company of ordinary people. And don't think you know it all!

Never pay back evil with more evil. Do things in such a way that everyone can see you are honorable. Do all that you can to live in peace with everyone.

ROMANS 12:14-18

WHEN YOUR PRODIGAL NEEDS PROTECTION . . .

I'm not asking you to take them out of the world, but to keep them safe from the evil one.

JOHN 17:15

WHEN YOU DON'T KNOW WHAT
TO PRAY OVER YOUR PRODIGAL . . .

May you have the power to understand, as all God's people should, how wide, how long, how high, and how deep his love is. May you experience the love of Christ, though it is too great to understand fully. Then you will be made complete with all the fullness of life and power that comes from God.

EPHESIANS 3:18-19

WHEN YOU NEED TO CHOOSE YOUR
BATTLES WITH YOUR TEEN WISELY . . .

Do all that you can to live in peace with everyone.

ROMANS 12:18

WHEN YOU NEED TO HEAR YOUR
CHILDREN ARE NEVER BEYOND GOD'S REACH . . .

Listen! The LORD's arm is not too weak to save you, nor is his ear too deaf to hear you call.

ISAIAH 59:1

Protection ⟶

WHEN YOU DOUBT IF GOD CARES ABOUT YOUR FAMILY . . .

The LORD himself watches over you!
 The LORD stands beside you as your protective
  shade.
The sun will not harm you by day,
 nor the moon at night.

The LORD keeps you from all harm
 and watches over your life.
The LORD keeps watch over you as you
  come and go,
 both now and forever.

PSALM 121:5-8

WHEN YOU NEED TO HEAR THAT
THE LORD WILL FIGHT FOR YOU . . .

Moses told the people, "Don't be afraid. Just stand still
and watch the LORD rescue you today. The Egyptians
you see today will never be seen again. The LORD
himself will fight for you. Just stay calm."

EXODUS 14:13-14

WHEN YOU NEED A PLACE OF REFUGE . . .

The LORD is good,
 a strong refuge when trouble comes.
 He is close to those who trust in him.

NAHUM 1:7

Provision ⟶

The English word *provision* might be translated "pre-vision." It means "to see beforehand." That's what God promises us. He sees the future, and He has already made a way before we even realize that a need is coming. It comforts me to know that God sees things before I do and that nothing takes God by surprise. Whatever you are facing, you can trust in Jehovah-Jireh, your Provider. His "pre-vision" becomes your provision. He has gone before you and made a way long before you even knew the way would be blocked. The next time you find yourself confronted with a difficult situation, thank God that He has already been there and has already made a way for you. Thank Him for His "pre-vision," then ask Him to show you His provision.

WHEN YOU'RE WONDERING WHERE THE PROVISION WILL COME FROM . . .

Don't worry about these things, saying, "What will we eat? What will we drink? What will we wear?" These things dominate the thoughts of unbelievers, but your heavenly Father already knows all your needs. Seek the Kingdom of God above all else, and live righteously, and he will give you everything you need.

Don't worry about tomorrow, for tomorrow
will bring its own worries. Today's trouble is
enough for today.

MATTHEW 6:31-34

This same God who takes care of me will supply all
your needs from his glorious riches, which have been
given to us in Christ Jesus.

PHILIPPIANS 4:19

**WHEN YOU NEED TO TEACH YOUR
CHILDREN A SIMPLE TRUTH ABOUT TRUST . . .**

The LORD hears his people when they call to him
    for help.
    He rescues them from all their troubles.

PSALM 34:17

Refreshment

WHEN YOUR SOUL NEEDS TO BE REFRESHED . . .

My child, don't lose sight of common sense and
discernment. Hang on to them, for they will refresh
your soul."

PROVERBS 3:21-22

**WHEN YOUR CHILD NEEDS TO UNDERSTAND
THAT REPENTANCE LEADS TO REFRESHMENT . . .**

Repent of your sins and turn to God, so that your sins
may be wiped away.

ACTS 3:19

**WHEN YOU NEED TO KNOW THAT
YOUR WORDS CAN BRING LIFE TO YOUR FAMILY . . .**

Your love has given me much joy and comfort, my
brother, for your kindness has often refreshed the
hearts of God's people.

PHILEMON 1:7

**WHEN YOUR MOTHER-HEART NEEDS TO KNOW
THAT REFRESHMENT IS COMING . . .**

The generous will prosper;
 those who refresh others will themselves be refreshed.

PROVERBS 11:25

**WHEN YOU NEED THE REFRESHMENT THAT
ONLY COMES FROM GOD . . .**

I have given rest to the weary and joy to the sorrowing.

JEREMIAH 31:25

Regret

Regrets are the fruit of poor choices. Maybe we regret not
going to visit Uncle Jack before he passed away. Or we regret a

choice made on a warm summer evening with a boy we thought we loved. Maybe we regret harsh words spoken and a friendship broken beyond repair. One meaning buried in the origins of the word *regret* is "to bewail the dead." It's okay to feel remorse over wrongs done and to feel sad over things that might have been. But those things are over now. They're dead. Bury each one. Mark each one with a headstone as a place of remembrance to not go back and make that same mistake again. But don't keep digging them up. Every day is a new beginning in God, and you have the opportunity to make new and right decisions today instead of lingering over wrong decisions made yesterday or thirty years ago. If you need to ask forgiveness, do it. If you need to repent of sin, do it. If you need to say you're sorry, don't delay. But then get up and dust yourself off. Purpose today to make the most of a clean slate and a new beginning in Christ—and allow your children to see you living in forgiveness out from under condemnation.

WHEN YOU NEED TO HEAR HIS HEART TOWARD YOU . . .

I have swept away your sins like a cloud.
    I have scattered your offenses like the morning mist.
Oh, return to me,
    for I have paid the price to set you free.
    ISAIAH 44:22

WHEN YOUR CHILD HAS BEEN CAUGHT IN SIN . . .

The sacrifice you desire is a broken spirit.
    You will not reject a broken and repentant heart,
      O God.
    PSALM 51:17

He has removed our sins as far from us
   as the east is from the west.
   PSALM 103:12

I—yes, I alone—will blot out your sins for my own sake
   and will never think of them again.
   ISAIAH 43:25

Releasing Children

I remember talking with a friend just a few weeks before my first-born was to be married. I was consumed with uncertainty and doubt about the situation. His wise words have resonated with me from that day until this: "You've raised your daughter. You've prayed over her. You've taught her well. Now trust the Holy Spirit in her and give her wings to fly." The Bible says that children are like arrows. Arrows serve no purpose safely tucked away in our quiver. To be effective, arrows must be launched. We have to let them go. If you've ever shot a bow and arrow, you know that as you pull that string back, the tension gets higher and higher just before you loose the arrow. So too in our lives the tension can be high in our children's teenage years. But in the end we can't let our fears outweigh our faith. We are called to raise our children well . . . and then release them. They were never really ours in the first place. We've simply had them on loan from Him who loves them even to the point of death on the cross. Begin now when your children are young to entrust them to the hands of the One who created them. Releasing our children is the natural order of things . . . and the time when you'll see all the seeds that you've so lovingly planted begin to bear fruit.

WHEN YOU NEED A REMINDER TO
SEND YOUR CHILDREN INTO THE WORLD . . .

Children born to a young man
    are like arrows in a warrior's hands.
How joyful is the man whose quiver is full of them!
    He will not be put to shame when he confronts his
        accusers at the city gates.

PSALM 127:4-5

WHEN IT'S BEEN A WHILE SINCE
YOU PRAYED FOR YOUR ARROWS . . .

Rejoice in our confident hope. Be patient in trouble, and keep on praying.

ROMANS 12:12

WHEN YOUR ADULT CHILD NEEDS TO HEAR WHAT GOD CAN DO . . .

My enemies did their best to kill me,
    but the LORD rescued me.
The LORD is my strength and my song;
    he has given me victory.
Songs of joy and victory are sung in the camp of
        the godly.
    The strong right arm of the LORD has done
        glorious things!

PSALM 118:13-15

All glory to God, who is able, through his mighty power at work within us, to accomplish infinitely more than we might ask or think. Glory to him in the church and in Christ Jesus through all generations forever and ever! Amen.

EPHESIANS 3:20-21

Rest

I'm a doer. I'm a goer. I'm an organizer. I'm an achiever. My family will tell you that I can be like a force of nature when I'm on a mission. Rest is not my default position. And yet God calls us to a life of balance. Even Jesus stepped aside and out of the frenzied crowds in order to recharge His batteries and renew His spirit. We weren't made to be "human doings." We were made to be "human beings," and sometimes we have to simply "be" for a little while. If your default is rest, perhaps you need to get a planner, set some goals, and define some concrete steps to achieve those goals. But if you're a doer like me, schedule rest. Schedule time for prayer. Schedule a getaway—even if it's just for a day. Schedule time to step away from the "busy" with your husband to talk, dream, and imagine. On the seventh day, even God Himself rested from His creative miracles. He defined for us a Sabbath day for rest from the busyness of life. Give yourself the gift of rest, busy mom. Your body, your mind, and your soul need it.

WHEN HIS YOKE IS THE ONE YOU NEED . . .

Jesus said, "Come to me, all of you who are weary
and carry heavy burdens, and I will give you rest. Take
my yoke upon you. Let me teach you, because I am
humble and gentle at heart, and you will find rest for
your souls. For my yoke is easy to bear, and the burden
I give you is light."

   MATTHEW 11:28-30

WHEN SLEEP SEEMS HARD TO FIND . . .

It is useless for you to work so hard
   from early morning until late at night,
anxiously working for food to eat;
   for God gives rest to his loved ones.

   PSALM 127:2

WHEN YOU NEED TO BE REMINDED
THAT THIS SEASON IS NOT FOREVER . . .

Be truly glad. There is wonderful joy ahead, even
though you must endure many trials for a little while.

   1 PETER 1:6

Sleepless Nights

Sleep doesn't come naturally to me. I'm a planner, and I can be
a worrier. I make lists and outlines while others are sleeping. I
sometimes use those sleepless nights for God's purposes. I can
use that time to plan, or more profitably to pray. But I can also

simply get in the habit of not sleeping because I think I have too much that needs doing—too much that I wrongly think depends on me. My mind won't shut down.

If you can relate, I hope this helps: God wants to work the night shift for you. A friend once sent me a meme that said, "You might as well give your problems to God because He's going to be up all night anyway." The Bible says, "He gives to his beloved sleep" (Psalm 127:2, ESV). The Bible also says, "Ask, and it will be given to you" (Matthew 7:7, ESV). Have you asked God for sleep? It took me years to learn this simple lesson: ask for sleep. So often we have not because we ask not. Worse still, we simply form bad habits and make destructive assumptions: "I just can't sleep at night." When you have one of those sleepless nights, use it wisely. Spend time with God. He's up anyway. But don't get in the habit of staying up late. Your husband and your children need you tomorrow. Ask God to give you sleep, to give your body rest—and then allow your heart to trust Him enough to let go and rest.

WHEN YOU NEED TO BE REMINDED THAT
GOD DOES NOT SLEEP, SO THAT YOU CAN . . .

I look up to the mountains—
   does my help come from there?
My help comes from the LORD,
   who made heaven and earth!

He will not let you stumble;
   the one who watches over you will not slumber.
Indeed, he who watches over Israel
   never slumbers or sleeps.
   PSALM 121:1-4

WHEN YOU NEED TO KNOW THAT GOD
WILL PROTECT YOU WHILE YOU REST . . .

I cried out to the LORD,
> and he answered me from his holy mountain.

I lay down and slept,
> yet I woke up in safety,
> for the LORD was watching over me.
> PSALM 3:4-5

WHEN YOU CAN'T SLEEP BECAUSE OF WORRY . . .

Don't worry about tomorrow, for tomorrow will
bring its own worries. Today's trouble is enough for
today.
> MATTHEW 6:34

WHEN YOU NEED TO HEAR GOD'S HEART
IS THAT HIS CHILDREN WILL SLEEP WELL . . .

You can go to bed without fear;
> you will lie down and sleep soundly.
> PROVERBS 3:24

WHEN YOU'RE RUNNING YOURSELF RAGGED . . .

It is useless for you to work so hard
> from early morning until late at night,
anxiously working for food to eat;
> for God gives rest to his loved ones.
> PSALM 127:2

Special Needs

WHEN YOUR CHILD NEEDS MORE THAN YOU CAN GIVE . . .

He gives power to the weak
  and strength to the powerless.
  ISAIAH 40:29

WHEN YOU FEEL LIKE GOD ISN'T LISTENING . . .

In my distress I cried out to the Lord;
  yes, I prayed to my God for help.
He heard me from his sanctuary;
  my cry to him reached his ears.
  PSALM 18:6

WHEN YOU NEED TO KNOW THAT JOY IS COMING . . .

Dear brothers and sisters, when troubles of any
kind come your way, consider it an opportunity
for great joy. For you know that when your faith
is tested, your endurance has a chance to grow.
So let it grow, for when your endurance is fully
developed, you will be perfect and complete,
needing nothing.
  JAMES 1:2-4

**WHEN YOU START TO PANIC—AND YOU KNOW
GOD'S HEART SAYS, "STAY CALM" . . .**

The LORD himself will fight for you. Just stay calm.
  EXODUS 14:14

Thoughts ⟶

"A penny for your thoughts." My husband's words brought me back from someplace far away. I had been lost in my own thoughts. I blinked awkwardly, suddenly aware that I had not been present for the past half hour. The mind is a curious thing. We have thoughts. Some of them are our own conjectures. Some are divine flashes of insight or inspiration given by God. And some are planted by the enemy who knows us only too well. He ensnares us as we walk the familiar paths of worry. If we can get our thought life straightened out, it's amazing how much it improves our daily life. Life, in the end, is a series of choices. What to do. What to prioritize. How to act when no one is looking. But perhaps nothing changes our life outcomes more than our thought life. Paul gives us very specific instructions about how we should think—a prescription, if you will. He says, "Think about these things!" (Philippians 4:8, ESV) Read the full verse and make a list of the things we're encouraged to think about. Whenever your mind wanders to regrets, or fear, or sin . . . look over that list and ask God to help you redirect your thought life.

WHEN YOUR THOUGHTS BECOME A BATTLEFIELD . . .

You will keep in perfect peace
    all who trust in you,
    all whose thoughts are fixed on you!
ISAIAH 26:3

Dear brothers and sisters, one final thing. Fix your thoughts on what is true, and honorable, and right, and pure, and lovely, and admirable. Think about things that are excellent and worthy of praise.

PHILIPPIANS 4:8

Make every effort to respond to God's promises. Supplement your faith with a generous provision of moral excellence, and moral excellence with knowledge, and knowledge with self-control, and self-control with patient endurance, and patient endurance with godliness, and godliness with brotherly affection, and brotherly affection with love for everyone.

2 PETER 1:5-7

Victory

Victory and victim are two sides of the same coin. A Bible college professor explained it this way: "Each day brings us choices and opportunities. The decisions we make and the course we follow will either make us victors over the enemy, or victims *of* the enemy." Did you catch that? We are engaged in a war—a war with victims and a war in which there will be a victor. Thank God we have the Holy Spirit and the armor of God every time we go onto the battle-field. We have an enemy who, the Bible says, prowls about like a lion and seeks to destroy us . . . to make us his victim and to declare victory over us (see 1 Peter 5:8). But the Lord's strength is made perfect in our weakness. Did you follow that? When we're weak, we're in a perfect position to emerge victorious. That's when God's strength is made perfect. Mom, I want you to be victorious. I want you to experience victory in your life. I don't want you to be the victim ever again. Open God's Word and ask Him to show you how to fight each battle you face. Then invite Him to manifest His strength through your weakness. Every day is a battle, and our enemy is relentless. You be relentless too, mom.

WHEN YOU OR YOUR CHILD NEEDS A WIN . . .

Victory comes from you, O LORD.
May you bless your people.
PSALM 3:8

You belong to God, my dear children. You have already won a victory over those people, because the Spirit who lives in you is greater than the spirit who lives in the world.
1 JOHN 4:4

WHEN YOU FEEL ANYTHING BUT VICTORIOUS . . .

I have given you authority over all the power of the enemy, and you can walk among snakes and scorpions and crush them. Nothing will injure you.
LUKE 10:19

Waiting

I've watched each of my now-adult children go through a season of what we've lovingly called "dangling." This is that awkward time when they're finished with high school and are seeking God's will for the next season of their life. It's awkward. It's not pretty. Waiting tries our patience. But wait. Didn't God say that patience was a fruit of the Spirit? (See Galatians 5:22.) Didn't He promise that those who wait upon the Lord will soar high like eagles? (See Isaiah 40:31.) The promises of God often come after a season of waiting. Perhaps you've heard the saying, "Lead, follow, or get out of the way." Or maybe you've heard the old maxim, "Don't just stand there—do something!" That's our natural bent. We're created to want to charge into every situation full speed. Waiting is uncomfortable. Dangling is awkward. Patience doesn't come naturally. No, it comes super-naturally. It comes from learning the truth of the old gospel hymn that says about God, "He may not come when you want him, but he's right on time." Practice waiting. Help your children learn to wait. God is faithful. He will give you direction if you don't grow impatient and plunge ahead in the flesh. Nurture the waiting process and look forward expectantly to God's provision. It's that kind of faith that pleases your heavenly Father.

WHEN WAITING IS THE HARDEST THING TO DO . . .

Wait patiently for the LORD.
> Be brave and courageous.
> Yes, wait patiently for the LORD.
> PSALM 27:14

I am counting on the LORD;
>   yes, I am counting on him.
>   I have put my hope in his word.
>   PSALM 130:5

WHEN WAITING TURNS TO WORRY . . .

Don't worry about anything; instead, pray about everything. Tell God what you need, and thank him for all he has done.
>   PHILIPPIANS 4:6

WHEN YOU NEED STRENGTH FOR THE IN-BETWEEN . . .

We also pray that you will be strengthened with all his glorious power so you will have all the endurance and patience you need. May you be filled with joy.
>   COLOSSIANS 1:11

Weariness

WHEN YOUR MOTHER'S HEART IS TIRED . . .

The Sovereign Lord is my strength!
>   He makes me as surefooted as a deer,
>   able to tread upon the heights.
>   HABAKKUK 3:19

WHEN REST IS NOT ON THE HORIZON . . .

He gives power to the weak
>   and strength to the powerless.
>   ISAIAH 40:29

Wisdom

We live in a world that equates knowledge with wisdom. A PhD from a prestigious school must mean you're very wise. Not so fast there, professor. The Bible says that knowledge apart from wisdom simply puffs us up and makes us arrogant. The Bible says we are to pursue wisdom. It also promises that if we ask for wisdom, God will give it to us. When my six-year-old gets stung by a bee, I need the knowledge of what to do about it to relieve her pain. Baking soda and Benadryl are my friends. But wisdom is what we need as wives and mothers. Even as children of the King we desperately need wisdom. Don't ever confuse knowledge with wisdom. A book or a website can give us knowledge, but a life devoted to understanding and pursuing God and seeking the fruit of the Spirit is the path of wisdom. Be wise, mom. The world needs God's wisdom, and He has chosen you as a way to share that wisdom.

WHEN YOU NEED TO HEAR GOD'S CLEAR INSTRUCTION...

If you need wisdom, ask our generous God, and he will give it to you. He will not rebuke you for asking.

JAMES 1:5

WHEN YOUR CHILDREN NEED TO KNOW THE IMPORTANCE OF CHOOSING GOOD FRIENDS...

Walk with the wise and become wise;
associate with fools and get in trouble.

PROVERBS 13:20

A wise woman builds her home,
> but a foolish woman tears it down with her own
> hands.

PROVERBS 14:1

Worry

The English word *worry* comes from a root word that means "to strangle or seize by the throat." I wish I could tell you I've never felt the stranglehold of worry. But that would be a lie. Are you a worrier, mom? Do you allow the enemy to seize you by the throat and strangle you? When we're being strangled, we can't praise God, we can't talk to God, we can't have a much-needed discussion with our husband. We lose our voice when we become strangled by fear. But the Bible says we can't add even a single day to our lives by worrying. To worry is to allow the enemy to silence us. In many ways, Satan's oldest lie was a temptation to worry. Even in the Garden of Eden, Satan's lie was simple: "You can't trust God. He doesn't have your best interests at heart. He's not going to do what's best for you." And isn't that the root of worry? We don't trust God. We don't believe He has our best interests at heart. We can't hand our concerns to Him, and we can't believe He'll do what's best. Worry is a symptom; lack of faith is the disease.

Whenever I find myself worrying, I remind myself of God's goodness and of His provision in times past. He has never failed me. He knows what is best, and He is working for my good. Stop worrying, mom. Get your voice back to speak hope and faith, to sing God's praises, and to speak life to your family. They need your steadying voice during times of trial.

WHEN MOTHERHOOD SEEMS TOO HARD . . .

Don't worry about anything; instead, pray about everything. Tell God what you need, and thank him for all he has done. Then you will experience God's peace, which exceeds anything we can understand. His peace will guard your hearts and minds as you live in Christ Jesus.

PHILIPPIANS 4:6-7

WHEN YOU NEED SUPERNATURAL
RELIEF FROM YOUR WORRIES . . .

Give all your worries and cares to God, for he cares about you.

1 PETER 5:7

WHEN YOU WORRY ABOUT THE FUTURE . . .

"I know the plans I have for you," says the LORD. "They are plans for good and not for disaster, to give you a future and a hope."

JEREMIAH 29:11

Yearning

WHEN YOUR HEART YEARNS FOR GOD . . .

As the deer longs for streams of water,
> so I long for you, O God.

PSALM 42:1

The LORD must wait for you to come to him
> so he can show you his love and compassion.
For the LORD is a faithful God.
> Blessed are those who wait for his help.

ISAIAH 30:18

**WHEN IT SEEMS GOD HAS NO PLANS
TO FULFILL YOUR LONGINGS . . .**

"I know the plans I have for you," says the LORD.
"They are plans for good and not for disaster, to give
you a future and a hope."

JEREMIAH 29:11

Don't worry about anything; instead, pray about
everything. Tell God what you need, and thank him
for all he has done. Then you will experience God's
peace, which exceeds anything we can understand. His
peace will guard your hearts and minds as you live in
Christ Jesus.

PHILIPPIANS 4:6-7

About the Author

Heidi St. John is a popular conference speaker, author, and blogger at *The Busy Mom*. Heidi speaks all over the country sharing encouraging, relevant, biblical truth with women. Heidi and her husband, Jay, are the founders and executive directors of Firmly Planted Family, an organization focused on family discipleship. The St. Johns live in Washington State, where they enjoy life with their seven children. When Heidi isn't homeschooling, babysitting her grandchildren, writing, traveling, or speaking, she can be found with her husband enjoying a cup of coffee and the view from their home in the Pacific Northwest.